D0970419

George Washington

George Washington

Lenny Hort

DK Publishing, Inc.

LONDON, NEW YORK, MUNICH,
MELBOURNE, AND DELHI

Designed for DK Publishing
by Mark Johnson Davies

Editor : Elizabeth Hester

Publishing Director : Beth Sutinis

Art Director : Dirk Kaufman

Creative Director : Tina Vaughan

Photo Research : Anne Burns Images

Production : Chris Avgherinos, Ivor Parker

DTP Designer : Milos Orlovic

First American Edition, 2005

06 07 08 09 10 9 8 7 6 5 4 3
Published in the United States
by DK Publishing, Inc.
375 Hudson St., New York, New York 10014

Copyright © 2005 DK Publishing, Inc.
Text copyright © 2005 by Lenny Hort
All rights reserved under International and
Pan-American Copyright Conventions. No part of this publication may
be reproduced, stored in a retrieval system, or transmitted in any form
or by any means, electronic, mechanical, photocopying, recording, or
otherwise, without the prior written permission of the copyright owner.

DK books are available at special discounts for bulk purchases
for sales promotions, premiums, fund-raising, or educational use.
For details, contact:

DK Publishing Special Markets
375 Hudson Street
New York, NY 10014
SpecialSales@dk.com

Published in Great Britain by Dorling Kindersley Limited.

Library of Congress Cataloging-in-Publication Data

Hort, Lenny.
DK biography : George Washington / written by Lenny Hort.-- 1st
American ed.
p. cm. -- (DK biography)
Includes bibliographical references and index.
ISBN 0-7566-0835-X (pb) -- ISBN 0-7566-0832-5 (plc)
1. Washington, George, 1732-1799--Juvenile literature. 2. Presidents-
-United States--Biography--Juvenile literature. I. Title: George
Washington. II. Title. III. Series.
E312.66.H67 2005
973.4'1'092--dc22   2004024076

Color reproduction by GRB Editrice, Italy
Printed and bound in the United States of America by
WORZALLA, Stevens Point, Wisconsin

Photography credits:
Front cover: Corbis/Richard T. Nowitz; Back cover: Owaki -
Kulla/CORBIS; Half-title page: Richard T. Nowitz; Full-title page:
Will & Deni McIntyre/Corbis

Discover more at
www.dk.com

Contents

Crossing the Delaware

December 25, 1776. It's Christmas, but the United States of America doesn't have a lot to celebrate. British troops have taken New York, and their German allies are camped comfortably near the national capital, Philadelphia. It doesn't look as if the new nation that broke from Britain on July 4 will live to see its first birthday.

George Washington has much to ponder as he rides a crowded boat across the icy Delaware River. Last year he'd been named commander in chief of American forces and been hailed as a great hero before he'd ever led an army into battle. Now Americans everywhere are wondering why they hadn't named a more experienced commander.

Just a few months ago, Washington had 19,000 troops,

but about the only skill they have shown is at running away from the British redcoats. Routed time after time, his army has shrunk below five thousand, and in just a week most of his soldiers will be free to go. What possible reason would any of them have for staying? Washington needs a victory, and he needs it now.

So Washington has planned a sneak attack, hoping to find the enemy groggy from Christmas celebrations. First, however, he has to get his men safely across the icy river and march them silently nine miles through the snowy darkness to the Hessian camp at Trenton.

If Washington's plan works, his army will live to fight again. If not, the new nation and its commander in chief are as good as dead.

chapter 1

Growing Up

February 22, 1732. Trains and planes and telephones have yet
to be invented. Only a dreamer might imagine electric lights,
flushing toilets—or an independent republic known as the
United States of America. At about 10:00 in the morning,
George Washington is born.

If anyone had dreamed that George would someday make
history, he or she might have
noted the exact time of his birth,
written eyewitness accounts,
preserved his diapers in museums.

During Washington's youth,
Britain and its 13 colonies would
challenge France and its
Canadian holdings for
supremacy in North America.

CANADA (New France)

New
England
Colonies

Middle Atlantic
Colonies

Louisiana (France)

Southern
Colonies

ATLANTIC
OCEAN

Florida (Spain)

But there was no reason to imagine that this boy was destined for greatness.

Washington was born in Virginia, the largest and richest of the 13 colonies. The American population was about 900,000 and steadily rising, and new arrivals to Virginia pushed the frontier back across the Blue Ridge Mountains and Shenandoah Valley, often at the expense of the Indian nations who had helped the first settlers to survive. There had been "starving times" when the first colonists had arrived, but by now the average American was better off than most people living anywhere else in the world.

The 1730s were a peaceful break in a long series of wars fought by Britain, France, and Spain over control of the New World. In those days, it took at least a month to sail the Atlantic, and King George II mostly allowed his American subjects to rule themselves. Members of the Washington family, including George himself, would serve in the House of Burgesses, Virginia's elected assembly.

The Washingtons had arrived in Virginia with George's great-grandfather in 1657. The Washington men seldom lived past their forties, but they packed a lot into their short lives.

Washington's Birthday

In 1752, the British Empire replaced the ancient Julian calendar with the Gregorian calendar we still use today. All dates got bounced by 11 days, and New Year's Day was moved from March to January. So though Washington was actually born on February 11, 1731, his birthday became February 22, 1732.

PLANTATION

A plantation is a farm, especially a large farm where slaves or hired workers live and raise cash crops.

Well-placed marriages and shrewd land purchases helped generations of Washingtons rise up through Virginia society. George's father, Augustine "Gus" Washington, had three children by his first wife. Soon after she died, Gus married an orphaned heiress.

Mary Ball was 23, which in those days was shockingly old to be a bride for the first time, but she did have a good-sized inheritance. Gus and Mary were living in a four-room house at Pope's Creek in Westmoreland County when her first child, George, was born. He was probably named after Mary's guardian, though he may have been named after King George.

We don't know a great deal about George's early childhood. While big brothers Lawrence and Augustine went to school in England, younger siblings Betty, Samuel, Jack, and Charles all arrived, older sister Jane died, and baby sister Mildred was born and died. The family prospered, and when George was three they moved to a 2,500-acre plantation later known as Mount Vernon. Four years later, they moved again to Ferry Farm on the Rappahannock River to be near an iron mine

The house where Washington was born burned down at least 200 years ago. The reconstructed house on the site that serves as a museum and visitors' center is probably larger than the original.

Gus owned. Lawrence, now grown, returned to Virginia and was named a captain in an American regiment of the British army. Little George hardly knew his older brother yet, but he was already looking up to him and probably dreaming of wearing a British uniform himself one day. Lawrence's adventures raiding a Spanish stronghold in South America made an exciting story for his adoring brother—even if the campaign itself was a disaster.

Mary Ball Washington's bossiness may have driven her son George to spend as much time away from home as he possibly could.

> ## *"Cleanse not your teeth with the table cloth, napkin, fork, or knife...."*
>
> — "Rules of Civility"

Meanwhile, Gus Washington built up the family fortune. He traveled a great deal to look after his far-flung tobacco plantations and business ventures, and George probably saw little of him before Gus's sudden death when George was 11. The famous story about how little George couldn't tell a lie to his father probably isn't true. No one can prove that George never whacked a cherry tree with a hatchet, but if he did, Gus may well not have been there to notice.

Gus had amassed at least 10,000 acres and 50 slaves in his 49 years. His will left the largest share, including Mount Vernon, to Lawrence. Augustine Jr. received the Pope's Creek plantation, while George inherited 10 slaves and the rocky soil of Ferry Farm, where he lived with his mother and four younger siblings. Ferry Farm was comfortable but crowded, with 13 beds in 6 rooms. The Washingtons never went hungry, but money was often tight, and George's mother would complain of poverty for the rest of her life.

Mary Ball Washington surely loved her son George, but she was bossy and hard to get along with. For much of her long life she seems to have been not so much proud of George's success as disappointed that he let such minor duties as being president and commander in

ARISTOCRAT

An aristocrat is a member of a high-born family.

chief get in the way of personally seeing to her every need.

George Washington may have had less schooling than any other president. He had expected to follow his half brothers to boarding school in England, but those plans died with his father. George appears to have had a mix of home tutoring and attendance at one or more church-run grammar schools. Some of his notebooks survive to show his skillfully penned lessons in math, geography, history, and astronomy.

George was also learning how to be a proper young gentleman. When he was about 15 he copied down 110 "Rules of Civility and Decent Behaviour in Company and Conversation," such as "Think before you speak," "Undertake not what

Ferry Farm went through several fires. The oldest surviving building on the property was built over 100 years after Washington moved out.

Young George was introduced to gracious living during his frequent visits to Belvoir, the Fairfax mansion, just a few miles from his brother Lawrence's home at Mount Vernon.

you cannot perform, and be careful to keep your promise," and "Being set at meat, scratch not, neither spit, cough, or blow your nose except there's a necessity for it."

The teenaged George seems not to have cared much for living under his mother's thumb, and he spent more and more time visiting friends and relations. Lawrence always welcomed George, and Mount Vernon became his home away from home. Lawrence was coming up in the world. He was named adjutant general—the commanding officer—for the Virginia militia, and he married his neighbor, Anne Fairfax, opening new doors for himself and his brother.

The Fairfaxes were genuine English aristocrats and one of the most powerful families in

MILITIA

A militia is a group of part-time soldiers who hold civilian jobs but can be called up to serve during emergencies.

Virginia. William Fairfax, Anne's father, advised the governor and managed the five million Virginia acres that his cousin Thomas, Lord Fairfax, had inherited. Their mansion, Belvoir, was far larger and more lavish than Ferry Farm or even Mount Vernon, and it bustled with fox hunts by day and dancing by night. One day George Washington would fight the British, but as a teenager he longed to be part of their world.

George made a strong impression on Lawrence's in-laws. Anne's brother, George William Fairfax, became one of George Washington's best friends, and her father took a special interest in advancing Washington's career. Knowing the boy's fascination with the military, William Fairfax pulled strings to get him an appointment as a midshipman—an officer trainee in the Royal Navy. George's bags were all packed before he finally listened to his mother's pleas and turned down the navy job.

George was introduced to the cream of high society at Belvoir, but he also got his first taste of frontier life when George William Fairfax invited him to join a team

Lawrence Washington had an enormous influence on his younger half brother George.

surveying Fairfax land in the Shenandoah Valley. The two Georges weren't used to roughing it. Washington's journal complained about the lice, the bedding, and the comical ignorance of the natives and settlers he encountered. As soon as food ran low, the friends abandoned the surveyors and hightailed it back to Belvoir. Pampered George Fairfax had had quite enough of the simple life, but George Washington would return time and again to the back country.

Washington owned this handsome field compass, which he may have used to determine directions and distances when surveying for the Fairfaxes.

Washington knew he'd never have the aristocratic life he craved working Ferry Farm. But with so many new towns being built and so many new settlers pushing the frontier, surveyors were very much in demand. The Fairfaxes got him a job helping to survey the new town of Alexandria, just a few miles up the Potomac River from Mount Vernon, then helped him to go into business on his own. Washington earned a good living surveying the Shenandoah Valley, and by the time he was 18, he had made enough money to buy up 1,459 acres on Bullskin Creek.

George Washington was a handsome, well-connected young man with reddish brown hair and

SURVEYOR

A surveyor measures and marks the boundaries of property.

16

blue-gray eyes, and his height of over six feet made him stand above the crowd. It would be years before false teeth stiffened up his winning smile. Still, George was not a hit with the ladies. He wrote about his "troublesome passion" for an unnamed "Low Land Beauty," and he wrote mushy poems about how his heart "lays bleeding every hour for her that's pitiless of my grief and woes." He twice proposed marriage to wealthy Betsy Fauntleroy and was twice rejected.

The woman he loved most of all was Sally Cary Fairfax, but proposing to her was out of the question—she was George Fairfax's wife. Two years older than Washington, dark-eyed, sharp-witted Sally would captivate him for many years. They danced and flirted and exchanged passionate letters. There's no evidence that their relationship ever went beyond that, yet when Washington was 66, the retired president would write her that "so many important events have

Washington's years as a surveyor paid well and provided the future commander with valuable experience at scouting out dangerous territory and living off the land.

occurred, and such changes in men and things have taken place....None of which events, however...have been able to eradicate from my mind the recollections of those happy moments, the happiest in my life, which I have enjoyed in your company."

Love was not the only worry on young George's mind. Lawrence had a cough he just couldn't shake, and month by month, year by year, he began to waste away. It was consumption—the disease we now know as tuberculosis. A trip to England and its renowned doctors couldn't cure him, and visits with George to warm springs in what is now West Virginia offered only temporary relief.

As the disease worsened, the brothers sailed together for the tropical Caribbean breezes of Barbados. George Washington's only trip beyond the future boundaries of the United States was a memorable one, though he seldom talked about it later. He saw dolphins and barracudas, weathered storms at sea, even attended the play that began a lifelong love of theater. And while Lawrence continued his battle with tuberculosis, George came down with smallpox.

Smallpox was one of the deadliest killers the human race had ever faced. As many as one in three victims died painfully within weeks, and survivors often had their faces permanently scarred. Washington was fortunate enough to recover with lifelong immunity and only a few faint scars on his nose. But he can't have felt very lucky at the time—despite doctors' reassurances, Lawrence's condition kept getting worse.

The two brothers agreed to split up. George sailed back to Virginia to take care of family business, while Lawrence headed for Bermuda, hoping against hope to find a climate that would heal his lungs. He didn't. Lawrence returned to Mount Vernon in June of 1752 and died a few weeks later, at age 34. George was no stranger to death, but the loss of his brother may have been the hardest loss of all.

The Washington brothers had to sail for almost five weeks to reach the island of Barbados, which was a British colony from 1627 until gaining independence in 1966.

The French and Indian War

Given how much George admired Lawrence, it was no wonder that he applied for his brother's position as head of the Virginia militia. George was bright and hard-working and an excellent horseman. Why should a total lack of military experience stand in his way?

Adjutant General might be too much responsibility for an inexperienced 20-year-old, but Governor Robert Dinwiddie was impressed enough to make Washington a major and put him in charge of the militia for a district covering about a quarter of Virginia. A militia command paid well, and with the colonies at peace, the duties were light. Every few months, volunteers got together with their friends and had fun parading around, taking target practice, and partying. But Washington's job was about to get a lot tougher.

Governor Dinwiddie hoped to expand Virginia into Indian territory in the Ohio River Valley, where there were big profits to be made trading furs and land. The Shawnee, Mingo, Lenape, and other tribes who lived there had other ideas. France, too, had designs on the Ohio. With the French moving south from Canada and Virginians moving northwest across the Allegheny Mountains, the stage was set for trouble.

When George II asked Governor Dinwiddie to order the French out of the Ohio Valley, young Major Washington volunteered to deliver the message. Washington didn't speak French, but his frontier experience and good connections made him a natural choice. His orders included scouting out French forces near the strategic forks of the Ohio—present-day Pittsburgh—where the Allegheny and Monongahela rivers joined. It was a dangerous mission through uncharted mountains and forests.

Washington set out in October 1753 with fur trader Christopher Gist as his guide. Gist led Washington to Indian villages to line up support for the British. Some tribes had old ties with England, and some with France, but few wanted to risk ending up on the losing side. Most Indians were happy to trade for guns and other supplies, and the English offered better, cheaper goods than the French— but they also sent more settlers and soldiers to take away tribal lands.

Tanacharison, a widely respected Seneca sachem,

Washington was about 40 when he dressed up in his French and Indian War uniform for his earliest known portrait.

Iroquois

The six nations of the Iroquois League—the Cayuga, Mohawk, Oneida, Onondaga, Seneca, and Tuscarora—were based in northern and central New York but dominated many other native peoples in northeastern America.

or chief, who had old scores to settle with the French—Frenchmen had reportedly slaughtered, boiled, and eaten his father—joined Washington in pressing north through the woods with Dinwiddie's letter.

The French officers greeted them with great courtesy. They promised to pass the English demand along to the French governor, Marquis Duquesne, but made it clear that they were not about to abandon their new forts or withdraw their troops.

Christopher Gist grew up in Baltimore society but became a skilled frontiersman.

His mission completed, Washington started back home through the wintry wilderness. He was fortunate to survive being shot at by an Indian guide and tumbling from a raft into the icy Monongahela before making his way to the colonial capital at Williamsburg. Washington presented his report to Governor Dinwiddie, who had it published on both sides of the Atlantic. The 21-year-old major was becoming famous.

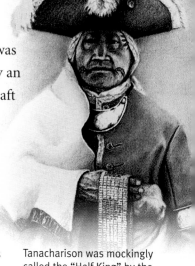

Tanacharison was mockingly called the "Half King" by the English, who were used to the commands of European monarchs rather than the complex consensus building of Iroquois sachems.

Dinwiddie promoted Washington to lieutenant colonel, then told him to raise a small army and march two hundred miles through the wilderness to build a fort at the forks of the Ohio. Recruiting for an extended campaign was not easy, especially with the House of Burgesses uninterested in paying the troops. With no roads on which to drag their cannons and supply wagons, it was slow going for Washington and his 159 men. They were barely halfway when they learned that a thousand French soldiers had gotten to the forks ahead of them and built the mighty Fort Duquesne.

Tanacharison warned that a French attack was on the way. He and some Iroquois warriors joined Washington in

The Seven Years' War

The Seven Years' War (1756–63) wasn't the longest of the many wars England and France had fought since the Hundred Years' War (1337–1453), but the conflict drew in so many countries on four continents that it might as well have been called World War I. Fighting broke out two years earlier in America, where it became known as the French and Indian War. Washington's attack on Jumonville and his defeat at Fort Necessity are considered the first shots in the war.

ambushing 32 Frenchmen early the next morning. The French were routed, their commander, Ensign Jumonville, killed, and dozens were taken prisoner. It was Washington's first taste of battle, and he wrote to his brother Jack, "I heard bullets whistle and believe me there was something charming in the sound." But it was a troubling victory. The French prisoners insisted that they had been wrongfully attacked while on a peaceful diplomatic mission like the one Washington himself had completed.

Washington's soldiers, together with Tanacharison's Iroquois warriors, prepare to ambush a party of Frenchmen led by Ensign Jumonville.

Washington knew that he was in a dangerous situation. If he led a speedy retreat, the Virginians

Fort Necessity, which was burned by the victorious French, has been reconstructed as part of a national park in southwestern Pennsylvania.

might look cowardly in the eyes of their Indian allies, but he was far too outnumbered to attack Fort Duquesne. Not knowing what else to do, Washington set his men to build what he named Fort Necessity. He hoped English reinforcements would arrive before the avenging French army.

Tanacharison warned Washington that the little wooden stockade was badly designed and, predicting English defeat, withdrew his warriors. The French and their Indian allies attacked on July 3, 1754, led by the slain French commander's brother. Washington and his men fought bravely, but Fort Necessity offered little protection, and heavy rain spoiled most of their gunpowder as they were picked off one by one. The French were also low on powder, however, and they allowed Washington to surrender with a promise to withdraw his surviving men to Virginia. Washington would always insist that he didn't know it

at the time, but in the French surrender papers he signed, he confessed to assassinating an innocent diplomat.

The "Jumonville Affair" was a major embarrassment to the British. Most Indians, seeing the incompetence of the puny British war effort, went over to the French, and Englishmen mocked Washington's surrender as "the most infamous a British subject ever put his hand to." But Virginians saw Washington as a hero for having fought the French against overwhelming odds.

Officially, Britain and France were still at peace. Everyone knew that war was coming, however—the conflict history would remember as the Seven Years' War. Washington hoped his Virginia regiment would be taken into the British army, where he could learn from experienced officers, but instead the regiment was broken up. Deciding that the colonial militia was a dead end, Washington resigned, rented Mount

British general Edward Braddock falls as French and Indian bullets shatter the silence of the forest. Braddock's defeat was one of the worst disasters in the history of the British army.

Vernon and its slaves from Lawrence's widow, and turned his attention to farming.

Washington wasn't ready to give up on an army career. He kept on applying to be made a British officer, and kept on getting turned down. His chance came when General Edward Braddock arrived in Alexandria. Braddock was going to march on Fort Duquesne, not with a handful of untrained colonials, but with two crack regiments of redcoats—seasoned British soldiers. Washington had never seen professional fighting men like these. Braddock needed an aide who knew the territory, and he accepted Washington's offer to serve as a volunteer, promising to have Washington made a British officer once they had taken Fort Duquesne.

Slowly, Braddock's forces cut their way through the woods and over the mountains. Washington was impressed by the determination and discipline of Braddock's army, although he wished that the proud Braddock would listen to his advice and take on Indian allies as the French already had.

Redcoats

British soldiers were known as redcoats or lobsterbacks for the red uniforms they wore to avoid shooting at each other on smoke-filled battlefields. Most of the redcoats were well-trained, well-paid, battle-hardened volunteers who had signed up for life.

Two months into the trek, Washington was "seized with violent fevers and pains in my head" and had to be left behind, but he recovered enough to ride with pillows on his saddle and catch up with Braddock just 12 miles from the forks. They never made it to Fort Duquesne.

The next afternoon, July 9, 1755, Braddock's army was marching through a narrow clearing when shots and Indian war whoops sounded through the woods. Redcoats started falling, picked off by French and Indian snipers hiding behind the trees. Braddock and his troops were masters at facing down enemy lines on an open battlefield, but frontier fighting had caught them completely off guard. Washington had his hat shot off and two horses shot out from under

A frontier settlement is raided during the French and Indian War.

Frightened Virginia settlers plead with Washington for help in stopping Indian attacks.

him, but he was the only one of Braddock's officers to escape unharmed. Braddock himself, cursing his panicked men, took a bullet through his shoulder and into his chest. He died four days later, one of almost a thousand British casualties.

After Braddock's disaster, the British abandoned plans for taking the Ohio Valley to concentrate on fighting the French in Canada. Emboldened, France encouraged Indian raids right into Virginia. The colony would have to protect its settlers without help from the redcoats. Washington, now 23, was named colonel and commander in chief of the Virginia Regiment and told to raise over one thousand troops to defend the frontier.

Once again, Washington's soldiers were underpaid, undersupplied, and overworked. Any British officer outranked a colonial colonel, and the British kept commandeering his troops and supplies. Rivalries between colonies made it harder still to equip the Virginia Regiment. Each colony printed its own money, and Pennsylvania gunsmiths wouldn't take Virginia cash.

Every time a settler was scalped or a homestead torched, other frightened settlers abandoned their farms and came to Washington for help, but there was little his undermanned force could do to stop lightning-fast Indian raids on the Shenandoah Valley. Desperate for more support, Washington wrote to Governor Dinwiddie, "The supplicating tears of the women, and moving petitions from the men melt me with such deadly sorrow that I solemnly declare.…I could offer myself a willing sacrifice to the butchering enemy provided that would contribute to the people's ease."

It was a miserable time for Washington. Dinwiddie ignored his repeated threats to resign, and British authorities ignored his pleas for the one action that might stop France from sending hostile Indians into Virginia—a renewed attack on Fort Duquesne. Not until three desperate years had passed and the British had won key victories in Canada were they ready to have another go at the Ohio Valley.

Brigadier General John Forbes commanded an army triple the size of Braddock's—more than six thousand redcoats and colonials. Forbes's forces set off from Philadelphia in 1758 with Washington on the general's staff. The eager Washington couldn't understand why they were moving so slowly, building a brand-new road across Pennsylvania when Braddock had left behind a perfectly good one through Virginia. Washington, foreseeing another disaster, argued with his commander, but Forbes knew what he was doing. Determined to avoid Braddock's mistakes, Forbes bided his time while other British forces cut off French supply lines and formed new Indian alliances.

This time, when the redcoats approached the forks of the Ohio, there was no ambush. Forbes and Washington found Fort Duquesne abandoned and in flames. The French, facing certain defeat, had slipped away and would no longer threaten that corner of the British Empire.

Virginia was safe again, and Washington gave up army life, this time, he was sure, for good. His dreams of a career in the Royal Army hadn't worked out, but there was plenty to look forward to at Mount Vernon now that he was engaged to marry one of the richest widows in Virginia.

This map from 1755 shows the disputed Ohio Valley region at the start of the French and Indian War.

chapter 3

The Master of Mount Vernon

Martha Dandridge had married Daniel Parke Custis, the only surviving son of a wealthy miser, when she was 18. After her husband died in 1757, the 26-year-old Mrs. Custis was the rich and single mistress of the prophetically named White House plantation. She was also looking for a good stepfather for her two children and a good manager for her large estate, preferably in the same person. George Washington, a year younger and a foot taller than Martha, fit the bill.

We don't know much about their courtship. Perhaps they had met at a ball in Williamsburg while Daniel was still alive. Washington came calling at White House in

Martha Dandridge Custis was about 26 and still married to her first husband when this portrait was painted.

March of 1758. A week later, he was back with generous gifts for Martha's servants. Within two months, he had ordered a wedding ring, and Sally Fairfax was writing to tease him about his impending marriage. While marching with Forbes, Washington wrote back that he still loved Sally. But Virginia marriages weren't about love. They were about business and property and raising families.

Colonel George Washington woos the widow Martha Custis while her children, Jacky and Patsy, play with presents he has brought them.

Martha was not a flirt like Sally, but she radiated a gentle charm. A man could relax around her. And she brought the restless George peace he had never known. They were married on January 6, 1759, shortly after his return from the Ohio.

Washington was rich now. He bought new land and slaves and expanded the house at Mount

Washington the Candidate

Washington was elected to the House of Burgesses while still a militia commander, and he continued to serve after his marriage. During election campaigns, he would treat voters to fiddlers, dancing, and kegs of beer. He didn't usually face much opposition, though when he did, he was not above asking the local sheriff to help round up his supporters.

Vernon, which he later inherited after Lawrence's widow died. He also ordered clothing, books, and such toys as "a Tunbridge tea set…a bird on bellows…a turnabout parrot…a neat dressed wax baby" and "a Prussian dragon" from London for Martha's children, five-year-old John Parke "Jacky" Custis, and three-year-old Martha Parke "Patsy" Custis.

Martha was an overprotective mother, and for years couldn't bear to be apart from her children. Washington, not wanting to be a stern stepparent, wrote that it was his duty to be "generous and attentive." He was genuinely fond of Jacky and Patsy, though both would cause much anguish.

Patsy was sickly all her short life. She was only 17 when Washington wrote, "She rose from dinner…in better health and spirits than she appeared to have been in for some time; soon after which she was seized with one of her usual fits and expired in…less than two minutes without uttering a word, a groan, or scarce a sigh."

Jacky was a good-natured boy, but he was as lazy as Washington was energetic. Washington wrote to schoolmaster Jonathan Boucher about "my anxiety to have him fit for more useful purposes than a horse racer." Boucher wrote back that "I must confess to you that I never did in my life know a youth so exceedingly indolent [lazy]." Being born rich and always having slaves do everything for him hadn't exactly built character in Jacky.

Jacky Custis was four and sister Patsy was two when George Washington entered their lives.

Washington himself continued to work hard. Most days he rose before dawn, regardless of the weather, to supervise his farms. Other times he traveled to Williamsburg to take his seat in the House of Burgesses or returned to the Ohio Valley to survey and invest in promising western land. He had married into money, but though he enjoyed living the good life, he felt a responsibility to build up the Custis fortune rather than spend it down.

Over the years, Washington expanded his home at Mount Vernon from the modest one-and-a-half-story farmhouse of his boyhood to the commanding mansion it remains today.

The riches of Virginia came from two things we view very differently today—slavery and tobacco. The more land and African slaves a planter could buy, the more tobacco he could ship to England in exchange for the latest fashions and luxury goods from London. Washington was born and raised in a tobacco-planting, slaveholding family, and his friends and relatives and neighbors all believed in the slave system. Slowly, however, Washington began to have doubts.

Slaves like William Lee, the trusted valet who helped Washington all through the Revolution, almost seemed like part of the family. Almost, but not quite. You couldn't buy and sell your own family. Or could you? Historians have suggested that one of Martha's household slaves was actually her

A slave family works the cotton fields near Savannah, Georgia, in this photo taken around 1860.

younger half sister. There's no hard evidence that Washington fathered any of his slaves' children, but many respectable plantation owners, including Martha's father, did just that.

Julian Niemcewicz, a Polish author who greatly admired Washington and was a guest at Mount Vernon in 1798, wrote, "General Washington treats his slaves far more humanely than do his fellow citizens of Virginia." Yet Niemcewicz described Mount Vernon slave quarters as "more miserable than the most miserable of the cottages of our peasants." Poland was far poorer than America, but the author noted that "the condition of [Polish] peasants is infinitely happier." Slaves at Mount Vernon ate well enough most of the time, but Washington, like other masters, was so stingy with clothing for his field hands that they often had nothing but rags to wear.

Washington couldn't help but notice that most of "his people"—he seldom referred to them as slaves—didn't usually do their jobs very well. Why should they? Slaves had to work from sunrise to sunset, but with no chance for promotion, and no way to make a better life for their children, they had no reason to do their best. Washington

$150 REWARD.

RANAWAY from the subscriber, on the night of Monday the 11th July, a negro man named

TOM,

about 30 years of age, 5 feet 6 or 7 inches high; of dark color; heavy in the chest; several of his jaw teeth out; and upon his body are several old marks of the whip, one of them straight down the back. He took with him a quantity of clothing, and several hats.

A reward of $150 will be paid for his apprehension and security, if taken out of the State of Kentucky; $100 if taken in any county bordering on the Ohio river; $50 if taken in any of the interior counties except Fayette; or $20 if taken in the latter county.
july 12-84-tf
B. L. BOSTON.

Like the Kentucky slaveholder who published this poster in 1784, Washington advertised and paid rewards for the capture and return of slaves who escaped from Mount Vernon.

observed that a team of slave carpenters produced four times as many fence rails when he watched them as when he didn't. Slaves had every reason to give themselves time off from work by losing or breaking or stealing the tools Washington's overseers provided.

Tobacco was the cash crop that made Virginia planters rich, but Washington came to favor other crops that were better for the soil.

Masters could whip slaves to force them to work harder, and they could threaten to break up families or to sell uncooperative slaves to sweltering, backbreaking Caribbean sugar plantations. Washington took all these measures at first, but he was troubled by the cruelty. Over time he resolved that he would never sell any slaves without their consent, and he bought slaves he didn't need rather than split up families by taking only the ones he wanted. For most of his life, Washington would weigh the moral good of freeing his slaves against his responsibility to provide a good life for Martha and her children.

His decision to kick the tobacco-growing habit came more easily. Nobody would know for centuries that tobacco poisons people with cancer, but Washington could see that the Virginia practice of planting nothing but tobacco was poison to the soil, turning rich fields into barren ones. Washington began an elaborate, soil-enriching rotation of seven different crops and found that there was more profit in selling wheat and alfalfa locally than in shipping tobacco to London.

Although tobacco made Virginians rich, it also drove them deep into debt to British merchants who underpaid them for their choicest crops, then overcharged them for fashionable English goods. In 1768, Washington ordered an expensive new carriage from London: "To be made of the best seasoned wood and by a celebrated workman." The "chariot" was as handsome and elegant as he had imagined, but within months it was falling apart from shoddy materials and workmanship. It was one more reason for Washington to declare his own independence from Britain, just as many other Americans were starting to do the same.

Washington took pride in the horse-drawn carriages and coaches in which he and Martha rode.

chapter 4

Trouble Brews

Americans like Washington had served in the French and Indian War as loyal subjects of King George II and then his grandson George III, who was crowned in 1760. The war had ended in triumph, with France completely expelled from North America. But now the bills were coming due, and nobody wanted to be stuck with them.

King George III thought it perfectly fair to raise the money by taxing the colonies. His American subjects still paid lower taxes than his British ones. Why shouldn't the colonists chip in for the war that had made them safer? Colonists and their leaders had dodged Mother England's rules for over a century, and they were determined to dodge new taxes on sugar, tea, and printed

George III was a hardworking king who wanted to do what was best for his people, but a stubborn streak often led him to make poor decisions.

matter. From New England down to Georgia, people refused to buy British goods. Washington, who had already

PARLIAMENT

A parliament is a group of people chosen to make a country's laws.

cut back on purchases from London, was happy to join these boycotts. He wrote, "At a time when our lordly masters in Great Britain will be satisfied with nothing less than the deprivation of American freedom, it seems highly necessary that something should be done to…maintain the liberty which we have derived from our ancestors."

Perhaps the colonists rebelled precisely because they were English. England had a strong tradition of law and liberty. Even the most powerful British monarchs still needed the support of Parliament, the courts, and the people. England had beheaded one king and banished another during the 1600s. George III and his prime minister, Lord North, had backing in Parliament for taxing the colonies—but colonists didn't have votes in Parliament.

The taxes weren't really that steep, and friendly gestures from the king might have smoothed things over. Instead he sent redcoats. The situation boiled over on December 16, 1773, when protesters dressed as Mohawk Indians jammed onto three British ships and dumped 342 of crates of tea into Boston Harbor—the legendary Boston Tea Party. The king sent four thousand redcoats to blockade the harbor and end home rule in Massachusetts.

Coolheaded Washington disagreed with the Boston Tea

41

Party, but the British response outraged him even more, and he joined the House of Burgesses in protesting. When royal governor John Murray Dunmore tried to shut the Burgesses down, the delegates simply shifted their meetings to Williamsburg's Raleigh Tavern.

The 13 colonies, longtime rivals, began to put up a more united front. Washington was sent to the First Continental Congress in Philadelphia, where he voted with the majority to cut off trade with Britain. When Washington returned to Virginia, he also reluctantly returned to uniform, accepting command of the militia being raised to guard against any redcoat invasion. Governor Dunmore seized the militia's gunpowder, then grudgingly returned it. Things did not go so peacefully in Massachusetts, where General Thomas Gage,

The Boston Tea Party provoked a British crackdown so harsh that many Americans who had supported King George went over to the rebel cause.

the new British commander, sent troops to seize militia weaponry. The militia, warned by Paul Revere and others that the British were coming, resisted. Someone fired "the shot heard round the world," and dozens of rebels and redcoats fell in fighting at Lexington and Concord in April of 1775. The New England colonies were at war.

Continental Congress

The 13 colonies created the Continental Congress to speak for their common interests in 1774. The House of Burgesses chose Washington and six other delegates to represent Virginia. Each colony's delegation, or group of representatives, had one vote, and no important decisions could be made over any colony's objection.

When the Continental Congress met again a few weeks later, the colonies agreed to send troops to support the Massachusetts militia. But who should lead them?

Washington never spoke much at the Continental Congress, but his militia uniform spoke for him, reminding the delegates of his heroism in the French and Indian War. At 43, he was in prime condition. He might not be as experienced as the British commanders, but he was a man of good character, and he was widely respected back in Virginia, the largest colony. John Adams of Massachusetts, the fiery leader of the

John Adams

John Adams served America in Congress and on important missions to Europe during and after the Revolution. Adams greatly admired Washington's courage, honesty, and unselfishness, but he grew jealous of the way Washington was idolized and often clashed with him.

small group in Congress that favored American independence, saw that putting the quiet Virginian in command of the Continental army would make New England's war into America's war. With Adams's strong backing, Washington was everybody's choice for the command he hadn't asked for and would always insist he didn't want.

The new commander in chief refused to accept a salary. He warned Congress, "I beg it may be remembered by every gentleman in the room that I this day declare with the utmost sincerity, I do not think myself equal to the command I am honored with."

Washington sent Martha the news: "You may believe me my dear Patsy, when I assure you…that, so far from seeking this appointment I have used every endeavor in my power to avoid it, not only from my unwillingness to part with you and the family, but from a consciousness of its being a trust too great for my capacity." On June 23, 1775, Washington set out for Boston. It would be six years before he saw Mount Vernon again.

The new commander was an instant American idol. People who'd never met him named their babies after him before he had issued a single order. Congress voted him a gold medal and Harvard University awarded the unschooled general an honorary doctor's degree before he had commanded a single battle. Americans changed the words of the traditional English anthem from "God Save the King" to "God Save Great Washington."

Washington knew he'd need plenty of help and advice if he wasn't going to disappoint everybody.

Washington enjoys a rare quiet moment in Philadelphia before he departs to take command of the Continental army.

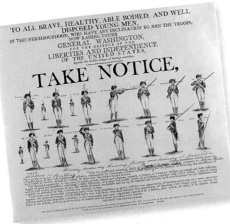

Posters like this one helped recruit volunteers for the Continental Army as well as local militias.

Charles Lee and Horatio Gates were veteran British officers who had served with Washington under Braddock. Both had settled in Virginia and gone over to the American cause, and Washington, hoping they could supply some of the experience he lacked, signed them on as generals.

Lee and Gates graciously accepted, though each thought himself more qualified for the top job than Washington.

While Washington and his generals rode to take command, the war didn't wait. New England troops killed or wounded more than one thousand British soldiers before being forced to retreat from Bunker and Breed's

Camp Chaos

Washington complained about having to break up fights among his rowdy troops. One witness told how a snowball fight at a Cambridge, Massachusetts, army camp turned into a brawl involving "more than a thousand combatants…with biting and gouging." Washington "rushed into the thickest of the melee, [and] with an iron grip seized two tall, brawny, athletic, savage looking riflemen by the throat, keeping them at arms length, alternately shaking and talking to them."

hills near Boston. After that costly victory, the British would fight more cautiously.

Still, Washington didn't like what he saw when he met his new army. Gunpowder was in perilously short supply. The soldiers were often drunk, and the stench made it clear that they didn't bother to use "necessities" (outhouses). Washington wrote, "Their officers generally speaking are the most indifferent kind of people I ever saw. I have already broke one colonel and five captains for cowardice....I daresay the men would fight very well if properly officered although they are an exceeding dirty and nasty people."

Nobody seemed to know just how large his army actually was, but clearly it wasn't big or disciplined enough to drive the British out of Boston. Most of the men were signed up for just six months. It would take longer than that to build a true American army.

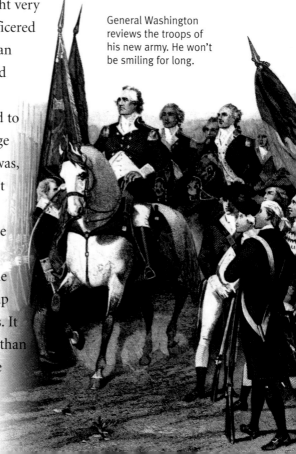

General Washington reviews the troops of his new army. He won't be smiling for long.

chapter 5

Revolution

The New England militias were not what Washington was used to in Virginia. He had never expected to see black soldiers. Some were freemen; others were slaves promised freedom in exchange for enlistment. Some units were all black, while whites and blacks fought side by side in others.

Washington's first instinct was to bar blacks, free or slave, from his army. He doubted that southern troops would serve beside them, and he feared that plantation owners would side with the British sooner than free their slaves. Then again, Washington needed all the soldiers he could get. Freedom was a powerful motivator, and there was talk that blacks might start fighting for the British. Washington decided to encourage black enlistment after all. Black troops would make up as much as a quarter of his army.

The war spread north and south. Benedict Arnold and Ethan Allen surprised the British and seized Fort Ticonderoga in northern New York, and Washington sent Arnold to attack British forces in Canada. Virginia wasn't spared. Governor Dunmore fled Williamsburg, then returned with British gunboats to bombard Norfolk. What was to stop him from leveling Mount Vernon? There was no telling when Washington would be home, and Martha accepted his invitation to join him at Cambridge, outside Boston, for the winter.

Washington hoped that King George would accept Congress's Olive Branch Petition offering peace. Instead the king told Parliament of plans "to put a speedy end to these disorders by the most decisive exertions." He hired an entire German army from the prince of Hesse-Cassel to help crush the rebellion. Hessian troops were the last straw for Washington and many others. What had started as a reluctant defense of old liberties became an all-out war to break free from what Washington now called "a tyrant and his diabolical ministry."

Phillis Wheatley

One woman who may have influenced Washington's decision to allow black troops was Phillis Wheatley, whose poetry had already made her the first African-American celebrity. The new commander was so moved by a poem Wheatley wrote about him that he invited her to call on him at headquarters. African slaves had served Washington for his entire life, but never had a black person been an invited guest at Mount Vernon.

As 1776 began, Washington needed to drive the British out of Boston before the new armies arrived. His troops outnumbered the redcoats, but they would be blown to

pieces by British artillery if they tried marching in. Where could the Continentals come up with guns to match?

ARTILLERY

Big guns such as cannons, mortars, and rockets, as well as the soldiers who use them.

Washington sent Henry Knox, his artillery commander, to Fort Ticonderoga, and Knox returned with 59 big guns that his crew dragged three hundred miles by boat, sled, and oxcart. Knox and three thousand men snuck the captured cannons up onto Dorchester Heights and got them into place in a single night. In the morning, the British stared up aghast at the guns trained down on them.

British general William Howe prepared to send his troops against Dorchester Heights, but a big storm postponed any

Hessian soldiers prepare to leave Germany after King George III has paid for them to go fight in America.

battles. By the time the storm lifted, Howe's plans had changed. Rather than sacrifice half his men storming the rebels' big guns, he abandoned Boston. The redcoats dumped most of their own cannons into the bay, then hurried onto ships and sailed away.

Washington raced his army to New York City to await Howe's next move, knowing that if the British gained control of the Hudson River, they could cut New England off from the rest of the colonies. Washington

British general Sir William Howe repeatedly beat Washington in battle but couldn't find a way to win the war.

fortified the city as best he could, but it was a daunting task. New York's islands lie in one of the world's largest harbors, but Washington had no navy to challenge the powerful British fleet and not enough troops to defend every landing site. Many New Yorkers were Tories—loyalists to the British crown—who would probably welcome a British invasion.

Some of Washington's officers urged burning the city to keep it from becoming a British base. It was good military advice. But Washington led a people's army, and he knew that the war effort was doomed without the people's support. He asked Congress for more troops, and hunkered down.

As spring turned into summer, there was still no sign of the British. Martha prepared to return to Mount Vernon. A growing majority in Congress now favored a permanent break from Britain, and on July 4, 1776, the Declaration of Independence was approved with not one colony voting against it. Only they weren't colonies anymore; they were states—the United States of America.

Five days later, the Declaration reached New York. Washington's officers read it to their cheering troops. A mob smashed a statue of King George himself. The lead statue

Members of the Continental Congress sign the Declaration of Independence in Philadelphia on July 4, 1776.

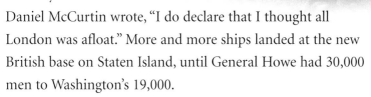

A New York City mob celebrates independence by toppling a statue of King George III.

was melted down for bullets. They would be needed soon enough—the British fleet had arrived.

Maryland rifleman Daniel McCurtin wrote, "I do declare that I thought all London was afloat." More and more ships landed at the new British base on Staten Island, until General Howe had 30,000 men to Washington's 19,000.

Howe took his time, hoping Washington would be sensible enough to surrender without bloodshed. Finally, Howe landed a large force on Long Island and outmaneuvered the Americans, taking one thousand prisoners and inflicting almost as many casualties before the remaining Americans fled to their fort at Brooklyn Heights. The British prepared for a siege of the Heights, but Washington managed to evacuate his 9,500 men and their artillery to Manhattan in a single foggy night. Washington himself caught one of the last boats, just as the British discovered that the Americans had slipped through their fingers.

Congress had instructed Washington to hold the city "at all costs," but the city could not be held. The Americans lost one skirmish after another, and thousands were captured when Fort Washington, their last Manhattan stronghold, fell. Across the Hudson River in New Jersey, Washington led his men out of Fort Lee just in time to escape the British, but the Americans had to abandon hundreds of tents and most of their cannons, food, and supplies.

Washington and his ragged army retreated across New Jersey, with Howe a step behind. To keep Howe from following them across the Delaware into Pennsylvania, the Americans seized every boat on the Jersey riverbank for miles around. The cautious Howe was content to let them go. The people of New York and New Jersey seemed ready to return to British rule. Washington's army had been reduced to a small fraction of its original size with minimal British casualties, and the war could be finished in the spring. Howe stationed British and Hessian units around New Jersey, then withdrew to New York for the winter.

The American commander's own staff had started to question his leadership. As Washington regrouped in Pennsylvania, General Charles Lee resisted

Charles Lee was one of Washington's most trusted generals at the start of the Revolution, but soon began to ignore his commander's orders.

the commander's request to bring his own forces across the Delaware. Lee wrote Gates that Washington was "weak to the last degree." That very day, Lee blundered into British hands. He had spent the night at a tavern miles from his army, and the British, alerted by Tory spies, arrested him.

Washington's most experienced commander was gone, and so was the bulk of his army. Most remaining soldiers were only signed up through the end of the year and eager to go home; unless a new army could be enlisted, he wrote his cousin Lund, "I think the game will be pretty well up." The only way Washington might persuade his men to stay on was to give them their first taste of victory. So he carefully planned a predawn Christmas raid on the 1,500 Hessians stationed at Trenton.

Hesse-Cassel and other German states sent around 30,000 troops to America. Although it wasn't their fight, the Hessians showed great courage in battle.

Almost everything went wrong with Washington's intricate battle plan. The Americans divided into three forces that were supposed to cross the Delaware at separate points miles apart, but only Washington's own group could get their boats through the ice floes. They were

Merry Christmas— Washington accepts the Hessian surrender at Trenton on the morning of December 26.

already hours behind schedule, making Washington "despair of surprising the town, as I well knew we could not reach it before the day was fairly broke."

Spies had warned Hessian commander Johann Rall that an American attack was coming, and he kept his troops on constant alert, canceling Christmas celebrations. Only the fierce winter storm that blew in on Christmas night finally made the Hessians let down their guard and get some much-needed rest. No army could possibly stage an attack in that kind of weather.

The sleepless, frostbitten Americans didn't make it to Trenton till after 8:00 in the morning, but, thanks to the blizzard, they still took the Hessians by surprise. Though the Germans roused themselves and fought back bravely, Knox's artillery overwhelmed them, and Colonel Rall was mortally wounded. The Americans marched nine hundred Hessian prisoners through Philadelphia.

Many of Washington's troops, their enlistments completed, were ready to go home. A sergeant later related the general's words to them: "My brave fellows, you have done all I asked you to do, and more than can be reasonably expected; but your country is at stake, your wives, your houses, and all that you hold dear. You have worn yourselves out with fatigues and hardships, but we know not how to spare you." Most of the men reenlisted, and they rang in the new year by surprising and defeating a British outpost at Princeton. Though the army was never again the size it had been in New York, what remained, bolstered by new recruits, was a proven fighting force.

Happy New Year—Washington's troops rout British forces at Princeton, New Jersey, on January 3, 1777.

chapter 6

Times That Try Men's Souls

Washington set up winter headquarters on the heights of Morristown, New Jersey. Here he could rest his weary veterans and train new recruits while keeping an eye on Howe's army in New York.

Although the area was surrounded by rich farmland, feeding and clothing the troops wasn't easy. The states wouldn't let Congress collect taxes to supply the army. Congress expected Washington to take whatever he needed from Tory farmers and shopkeepers, but the general felt people would be more loyal to an army that paid its own way instead of taking over homes like the redcoats or plundering farms like the Hessians.

The army had stayed fairly healthy while the soldiers were New Englanders fighting close to home. But the new mix of men from many states marching from town to town was a recipe for spreading diseases more deadly than British guns. Arnold's

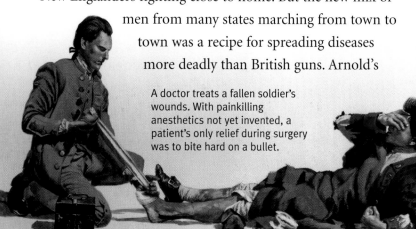

A doctor treats a fallen soldier's wounds. With painkilling anesthetics not yet invented, a patient's only relief during surgery was to bite hard on a bullet.

army in Canada had won a string of victories, only to be forced to retreat after being decimated by smallpox. Washington, immune to the disease since surviving it in Barbados, used the winter to inoculate all new recruits— to have them deliberately infected with very mild cases in order to stimulate their bodies' natural defenses.

Martha, herself reluctantly inoculated the year before, again joined her husband, as she would do

Medical Treatment

Getting cured in Washington's day could be even worse than getting sick. Standard practices included draining much of a patient's blood or giving medicines to force vomiting. Doctors didn't know about germs and antiseptics, so wounds that hadn't seemed deadly on the battlefield often became dangerously infected.

every winter throughout the war. "Lady Washington" kept Washington's spirits up in difficult times while helping with paperwork and entertaining important visitors. Some of the guests had traveled all the way from Europe.

Congress had sent beloved statesman Benjamin Franklin to Paris to line up France's help against its old enemy, England. King Louis XVI was uneasy about being drawn into another war, but he secretly sent much-needed money, supplies, and weapons to Washington at Morristown. French engineers trained the Americans to build stronger forts, while an ever-growing parade of French officers offered to

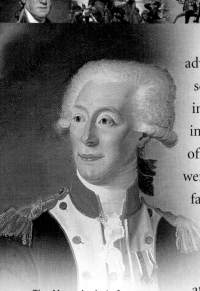

The Marquis de Lafayette was only 19 when Congress made him a major general, but Washington found him a skilled adviser in camp and a bold leader on the battlefield.

advise the general on tactics or to serve in high commands with interpreters translating their orders into English. Most of the French officers were more trouble than they were worth, but Washington took a fatherly interest in the young Marquis de Lafayette and grew to rely on him throughout the war.

In June 1777, the British attacked on two fronts. General John Burgoyne brought a large army down from Canada, retook Fort Ticonderoga, and advanced into the upper Hudson Valley. Meanwhile, General Howe marched his army in and out of New Jersey, hoping to lure Washington down from the Morristown heights and again humiliate him in open battle. Washington wouldn't take the bait, but when Howe sailed 18,000 men up Chesapeake Bay and marched toward Philadelphia, Washington had little choice but to defend the capital.

The Continental army paraded past an uneasy crowd mixed with patriots and Tories, then raced to take positions south and west of the city. Outmaneuvered by Howe, Washington suffered heavy losses at Brandywine, Pennsylvania, but withdrew with his forces mostly intact. Congress evacuated Philadelphia while Howe tried in vain to lure Washington's forces out in the open and crush them. Washington, learning from his disastrous defeats defending New York, was determined to choose his battles carefully. On September 26, the British entered Philadelphia with little resistance.

Just a week later, Washington staged a sneak attack on British troops at Germantown, Pennsylvania. Both sides lost hundreds of men in the inconclusive battle, but Howe, who had long considered Washington a "blockhead," gained new respect for the rebel leader who just wouldn't quit.

On the American side, however, doubts grew about Washington's competence. Even John Adams wrote that if Washington had been more skillful and less cautious, "he might have cut to pieces Howe's army." General Horatio Gates had beaten Burgoyne at

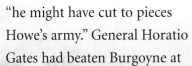

Redcoats and Americans both suffered heavy losses when Washington tried to duplicate his victory at Trenton with a raid at Germantown, Pennsylvania.

Saratoga, New York, taking five thousand British prisoners. Washington had never in his life won that kind of victory.

Washington, seeing no opportunity to dislodge the British from Philadelphia, chose winter headquarters 18 miles northwest at Valley Forge, Pennsylvania. His army, always poorly supplied, was more ragged than ever. Many soldiers faced winter hundreds of miles from home without blankets, coats, or shoes while Congress bickered with the state governments over whose job it was to feed and clothe them. While British officers danced with Tory beauties in the warm mansions of Philadelphia, Washington's men huddled in freezing tents until they could build themselves enough cabins. Albigence Waldo, a Connecticut surgeon serving with the Continental army at Valley Forge, wrote in his diary on December 14, 1777, "Poor food…hard lodging…Cold weather… fatigue…Nasty clothes…nasty cookery… I can't endure it….Why are we sent here to starve and freeze?"

More food started coming in after a few

Food, shoes, and warm clothing were in short supply as Washington's army wintered at Valley Forge.

Steuben trains American troops at Valley Forge.

months, and in February 1778 a German with a very long name arrived to transform the Continental army. Lieutenant General Frederick William Augustus Henry Ferdinand Baron von Steuben wasn't really a baron, wasn't really a lieutenant general, and didn't speak any English. But he was better at training soldiers than anyone Washington had ever seen. That winter and spring he taught the Continentals how to move and maneuver in formation, how to charge with bayonets—how to fight as a professional unit.

About two thousand American soldiers died at Valley Forge from starvation, cold, or disease, more than had been killed in all the past year's battles, yet the army left stronger than it had arrived. France had officially recognized the American nation and was sending more aid. General Howe, like General Gage before him, had been called back to London. When word came in June that Sir Henry Clinton, the new British commander in chief, was abandoning Philadelphia, Washington had reason to hope that the war

might soon end in American victory. Whoever could conquer London, conquered England, but nine months in America's largest city had done nothing for the British. Clinton decided to march his men back to the more strategically important ground of New York. Washington placed the reliable Benedict Arnold in charge of Philadelphia's defenses, then left Valley Forge to dog Clinton's retreat.

Sir Henry Clinton focused the British war effort on the American South and battled Washington as little as he possibly could.

Washington still hesitated to face the redcoats on open ground, but he kept looking for a chance to catch them off guard and do real damage. With the British lines stretched thin in central New Jersey, the time was right. General Lee had been freed in exchange for British prisoners, and Washington told him to lead an attack on British forces passing near Monmouth Courthouse.

Lee was a seasoned commander, but he panicked almost the moment the redcoats fired back at his men. Lee and his forces beat a speedy retreat, with a large British force in hot pursuit. General Charles Scott reported that Washington "swore...till the leaves shook on the trees." Washington and General Nathanael Greene rallied the Americans who, putting Steuben's training into action for the first time, held

COURT-MARTIAL

To court-martial is to put soldiers or sailors on trial before a military court of law.

off the redcoats in a bloody all-day battle. Clinton's troops stole away during the night and made it to New York without further incident. Washington was furious over Lee's cowardice and had him court-martialed and dismissed from the army.

The Battle of Monmouth Courthouse had been fought to a draw, but Clinton was impressed enough with the new and improved American army to avoid battling them for years to come. With neither side strong enough to defeat the other in combat, the commanders tried to win the war by other means. Washington looked to France to counter the powerful British navy while Clinton looked for American officers willing to betray their country.

Washington stops Lee's retreat and rallies American troops at Monmouth.

Espionage

Throughout the Revolution, Washington relied on an extensive network of spies ranging from farmers to merchants to washerwomen. The general used his spies both to scout out information on British plans and troop movements, and to feed the enemy false information and misleading rumors about his own army.

He found one in Benedict Arnold.

The courageous Arnold had been crippled defeating Burgoyne while Gates took all the credit, and he resented the way Congress kept promoting lesser talents over him. While serving in Philadelphia, Arnold married Peggy Shippen, a rich, beautiful Tory. Major John André, one of Clinton's top aides, had danced with her during the British occupation, and Peggy hooked him up with her husband. Arnold and André made secret plans for handing the British the key to the Hudson.

West Point commanded the cliffs over the Hudson River, and no British ship could get past its cannons or the enormous iron chain that stretched across the river. The fortress was so well gunned and positioned that any British attack would be suicidal—unless the Americans surrendered

Benedict Arnold, one of America's finest officers, stunned Washington by plotting to hand West Point over to the British.

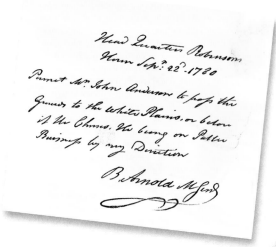

Sentries found this pass, signed by Benedict Arnold, hidden in Major André's shoe.

without a fight. Arnold had Washington's trust, and he convinced the general to put him in charge.

Washington arrived at West Point on September 25, 1780, for a routine inspection. He was looking forward to breakfast with Arnold and Peggy, but Arnold was nowhere to be found. He had escaped aboard a British warship, the *Vulture,* after learning that American sentries had searched and arrested a suspicious civilian calling himself John Anderson. It was really Major André in disguise, his shoe stuffed with papers pointing to Arnold's guilt. André was convicted and hanged as a spy after Clinton refused to swap Arnold for him.

Though Arnold's plot had been foiled, Washington was badly shaken by his old friend's treason and by the knowledge that one of his best officers would now be fighting for the British.

TREASON

Treason is the crime of deliberately betraying one's own country.

chapter 7

"It Will Not Be Believed"

Washington saw only scattered fighting for three whole years after Monmouth. The states still wouldn't let Congress collect taxes, so Washington had to fight on the cheap with an army too small to challenge Clinton's hold on New York. When he could pay his troops at all, it was with paper money that was worth less every day. Soldiers mutinied—revolted against their officers—in Pennsylvania and New Jersey, and it was harder than ever to keep the army together.

France sent a large fleet and a 5,500-man army across the Atlantic to help against the British, but the French general, Count Rochambeau, didn't seem interested in fighting. Washington appealed to Rochambeau to help launch a coordinated attack on Clinton, but the French fleet sailed to the Caribbean while the

All 13 states as well as the Continental Congress printed their own worthless paper money during the Revolution.

French army settled in comfortably at Newport, Rhode Island.

Clinton sailed southward. After a long siege he captured Charleston, South Carolina, taking five thousand prisoners of war. Benedict Arnold, now a British general, burned Virginia's new capital, Richmond, while British troops under Lord Cornwallis pressed inland through the Carolinas, crushing Gates's Continental forces. General Nathanael Greene countered, inflicting heavy British losses, but Cornwallis still had over nine thousand redcoats when he invaded Virginia.

Count Rochambeau and Washington didn't trust each other at first, but working together they defeated the British.

While Martha was up north with Washington in April 1781, British captain Thomas Graves aimed the guns of HMS *Savage* at Mount Vernon. Lund Washington, who managed the estate in George's absence, convinced Graves to spare the house in exchange for provisions. Seventeen Washington slaves took up Graves's offer of freedom and sailed off with him. General Washington understood why Lund had bargained with the British, yet he wrote his cousin, "It would have been a less painful circumstance to me to

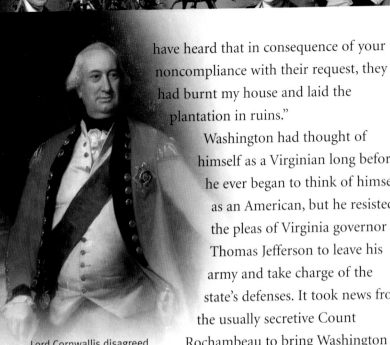

have heard that in consequence of your noncompliance with their request, they had burnt my house and laid the plantation in ruins."

Washington had thought of himself as a Virginian long before he ever began to think of himself as an American, but he resisted the pleas of Virginia governor Thomas Jefferson to leave his army and take charge of the state's defenses. It took news from the usually secretive Count Rochambeau to bring Washington home. The French general joined his forces with Washington's north of

Lord Cornwallis disagreed with King George's policies in America, but he loyally and brutally carried them out.

Manhattan and confided that a large French fleet would be sailing for Chesapeake Bay to harass British shipping. If the combined French and American armies arrived at the same time, Rochambeau suggested, they could seize British outposts. Washington took the count's simple plan and made it into something grander—a gamble at trapping Cornwallis's army.

Washington began feeding British spies false information of plans to invade New York's Staten Island. Meanwhile, Clinton's spies reported that the Americans were assembling landing craft on the Jersey coast and the French were building ovens big enough to feed an army. Clinton, who had returned to New York City, ordered Cornwallis to ship him two thousand reinforcements from Virginia. His forces reduced and harassed by Lafayette, Cornwallis dug his remaining troops into fortifications at Yorktown at the mouth of Virginia's York River.

The French and American troops marched south into New Jersey, believing as Clinton did that they would soon wheel around toward Staten Island. Instead they found themselves miles to the southwest at the Delaware River. Washington got them onto boats to continue on their way to surprise Cornwallis at Yorktown. Washington himself

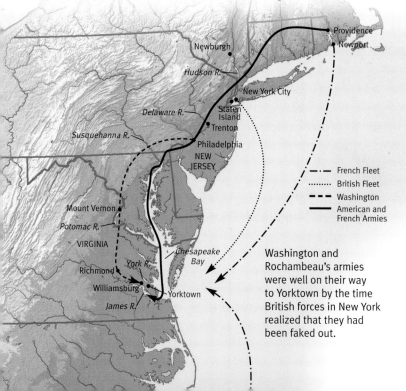

French Fleet
British Fleet
Washington
American and French Armies

Washington and Rochambeau's armies were well on their way to Yorktown by the time British forces in New York realized that they had been faked out.

The British surrender at Yorktown assured American independence.

Martha was there, and so were her son, Jacky, and his wife, Eleanor Calvert Custis, along with four grandchildren born since Washington had first ridden off to war. Jacky had sat out the revolution, but now he insisted on joining his stepfather. When they arrived at Yorktown, Cornwallis's fort was surrounded, with any possible relief cut off by the French fleet in Chesapeake Bay.

Rochambeau was an expert on siege warfare, and over the next three weeks his engineers' trenches reached closer and closer to Cornwallis's fort while American and French artillery battered the British defenses and British guns fired back. A Virginia private described how, "during a tremendous cannonade from the British," Washington took his telescope and "mounted the highest, most prominent, and most exposed part of our fortifications and there stood exposed to the enemy's fire, where shot seemed flying almost as thick as hail and were instantly demolishing portions of the embankment around him, for ten or fifteen minutes until he had completely satisfied himself of the purpose of the enemy."

The noose kept tightening until the British guns were silenced, and Cornwallis capitulated. On October 19, 1781, some eight thousand British soldiers filed out of the battered fortress. Sarah Osborn, who cooked and cleaned for the Continentals while married to a corporal, described how the British army "marched out beating and playing a melancholy tune, their drums covered with black handkerchiefs and their fifes with black ribbons tied around them." (The legend that British musicians played a tune called "The World Turned Upside Down" is probably too good to be true.) Cornwallis, too proud or too embarrassed to surrender personally to Washington, sent a general to hand over his sword. Washington returned the insult by having General Benjamin Lincoln, whom Clinton had humiliated at Charleston, accept it.

For the first time since the war had started, Washington felt he could take some time off, but his vacation wasn't a happy one—Jacky Custis had taken sick almost as soon as he'd arrived at Yorktown, then died at the age 27 a few weeks after the siege ended.

Washington didn't know it yet, but the war had seen its last major battle. Parliament didn't want to keep pouring

money into a losing cause. Lord North resigned as prime minister, and King George agreed to recognize American independence.

Washington told General Greene that anything historians wrote about the revolution would be regarded as fiction, "for it will not be believed that such a force as Great Britain has employed…could be baffled…by numbers infinitely less, composed of men oftentimes half starved; always in rags, without pay, and experiencing at times every species of distress which human nature is capable of undergoing."

General Clinton was replaced by yet another commander, as the

Washington made his headquarters at Newburgh, New York, during the final year and a half of the Revolution.

redcoats remained in New York City for two more years while peace negotiations dragged on. Washington had to keep his army together and close enough to keep an eye on the redcoats, but Congress and the states were less interested than ever in paying for it now that the British threat was over. Washington was told to send most of his troops home without the pay they had been promised.

Officers railed against "a country that tramples upon your rights, disdains your cries, and insults your distresses." Anonymous letters called on the men to

Treaty of Paris

John Adams (left) and Benjamin Franklin (center) spent many months in France negotiating a peace treaty to officially end the American Revolution. Britain recognized American independence and agreed to U.S. boundaries south of Canada, north of Spanish Florida, and east of the Mississippi River. The United States in turn agreed to honor old debts to Britain and restore property that had been confiscated from loyalists.

refuse to give up their arms until they were paid. Washington's officers urged him to take matters into his own hands. If Congress and the states wouldn't do what was right, then he should use the strength of his army to force them to pay up. If Washington wouldn't lead a military takeover, someone else would.

Washington was embarrassed about needing glasses, and many of his officers had never seen him wear them.

Soldiers weren't the only ones fed up with the weak, hopelessly divided government. Congress owed millions to merchants who had helped arm and feed the revolution. Such members of Congress as Alexander Hamilton, who had been one of Washington's top aides for most of the war, wanted Washington to force the states to give more power to the central government. American liberty was in danger, not from the British, but from its own defenders.

Washington called his officers together to ask them to be patient with Congress and not "open the floodgates of civil discord and deluge our rising empire in blood." Their response, at first, was chilly. Then Washington, whose leadership skills had always gone beyond choosing the right words, "made a short pause, took out his spectacles, and begged the indulgence of his audience while he put them on, observing at the same time that he had grown gray in their service, and now found himself growing blind. There was something so natural, so unaffected in this appeal," wrote Major Samuel Shaw, that the officers, their own eyes damp, set aside talk of a new revolution. When a peace treaty with England was finally signed, the troops went home with nothing more in their pockets than certificates from Congress promising to pay them when it could.

Washington, the most powerful and popular man in America, had brushed aside calls to become a military dictator, or even a king. He wrote to the state governments of his intention "to pass the remainder of my life in a state of undisturbed repose," and urged the states to set aside their own separate interests and create a strong national government that would keep its promises to the veterans.

The British left New York on November 25, 1783, taking many Tories with them. Washington made his good-byes to his few remaining officers, returned his commission to Congress, and arrived at Mount Vernon on Christmas Eve.

With independence won after eight long years, Washington and his officers prepare to go their separate ways.

chapter 8

A More Perfect Union

My Dear Marquis," Washington wrote Lafayette, "I am become a private citizen on the banks of the Potomac, and under the shadow of my own vine and my own fig tree, free from the bustle of a camp and the busy scenes of public life….Envious of none, I am determined to be pleased with all, and this my dear friend, being the order for my march, I will move gently down the stream of life, until I sleep with my fathers."

A private citizen? Not a chance. Mount Vernon had always hosted hundreds of guests every year, and now it was more crowded than ever with friends, veterans, and perfect

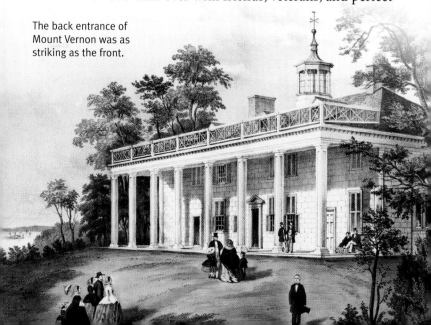

The back entrance of Mount Vernon was as striking as the front.

strangers determined to drop in on the most famous man in America. He wrote his mother, who was threatening to move in with him, that his home "may be compared to a well-resorted tavern, as scarcely any strangers who are going from north to south or from south to north do not spend a day or two at it."

Mules, born to a mother horse and a father donkey, can't have babies themselves. Washington is credited with introducing widespread use of mules to American farms.

The war had been costly for Washington. To set a good example, Washington accepted payment for his enormous expenses in the same worthless certificates the soldiers had been forced to take. He had to sell some of his western land to pay for upkeep and entertaining at Mount Vernon.

Farming became his passion, and people from as far away as China sent him seeds and cuttings. Most prized of all was a jack—a magnificent male donkey presented by the king of Spain. Washington hoped to breed Royal Gift with Mount Vernon's mares to produce superior mules, faster than donkeys but with more strength and stamina than horses. To Washington's frustration, the long-eared Spanish aristocrat showed no interest in mares. The determined general made a new battle plan. The high-born jack would be introduced to

Washington designed an ingenious 16-sided barn. Horses and mules circled inside, trampling grain so that wheat separated from chaff and slid through slits in the floor to a chamber below.

an American jenny—a female donkey. As soon as he was in the mood for love, the jenny retreated and a mare marched in. Once again, Washington's surprise attack won the day, and soon Mount Vernon had a majestic herd of mules.

Washington was 51 when the war ended. Although still in good health, he didn't think that he was long for this world. He had already outlived his father, grandfather, and great-grandfather. Washington still had his hair, which he usually kept stylishly powdered and tied back in a tight braid, but he was down to just one tooth, supplemented by assorted sets of dentures. No, he never used wooden teeth, and no, he never wore dentures made by Paul Revere. At various times in his life, however, he chewed with spring-loaded contraptions mounted with cow teeth, carved hippopotamus teeth, and human teeth. Washington was known to pay slaves who volunteered to have teeth yanked out and used in his dentures.

Maybe Washington's greatest disappointment was that he didn't have any children and, now that he and Martha were past 50, probably never would. Washington never wanted to admit it to himself, but he may have been sterile, perhaps because of smallpox or one of the other illnesses he had lived through. Jacky Custis's widow had remarried, but her two youngest children, Eleanor "Nellie" and George Washington Parke Custis, who was nicknamed "Wash" or "Tub," stayed on at Mount Vernon to be raised by Martha. Washington was devoted to Martha's children and especially her grandchildren, but to him, it wasn't quite the same.

Washington was also disappointed at news from around America. Nothing about the United States was united. The states continued to squabble with each other, and often didn't even bother to send delegates to Congress. Many states ignored terms of the treaty with Britain, and Britain in turn refused to budge from northwestern forts it had agreed to surrender. The army still hadn't been properly paid, and, like most of the disappointed soldiers, Washington sold off his certificates for about a twentieth of their official value. Massachusetts farmers, unable to pay their debts with the certificates, followed a Revolutionary War captain named Daniel Shays to take

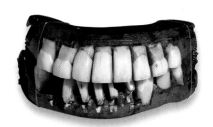

With false teeth like these, it's no wonder that Washington is seldom painted with a smile on his face.

up arms against state officials who tried to seize their farms.

Although the Massachusetts uprising soon petered out, reports of Shays's Rebellion troubled many Americans. Washington wrote John Jay, the U.S. secretary for foreign affairs, "Something must be done, or the fabric must fall. It certainly is tottering!" Still, Washington hesitated to take an active part in the growing movement to strengthen the national government. "Having happily assisted in bringing the ship into port and having been fairly discharged, it is not my business to embark again on a sea of troubles."

Just the thought of giving up his treasured retirement made Washington sick with worry, but duty called once again. He reluctantly let Virginia send him to Philadelphia in 1787. Congress had asked delegates from all the states to gather to propose changes to the Articles of Confederation—the guidelines that formed the loose alliance between the states. Washington's friends assured him that his return to public life would be brief, but he knew better.

James Madison, who is often called "the father of the Constitution," became one of Washington's top advisers and went on to serve as America's fourth president.

Washington was pleasantly surprised by the cheering crowds that greeted his arrival in Philadelphia. He was a guest in Robert Morris's mansion, which had been General Howe's headquarters during the British occupation. It would be a long stay.

The 116-day meeting of 55 men from 12 states (Rhode Island stayed home) came to be known as the Constitutional Convention. The delegates' first task was to pick a chairman. Once again, Washington was chosen by unanimous vote for a job he hadn't asked for. Washington did not take part in debates, but he met with delegates in taverns, parlors, and theaters, helping to cool tempers and quietly encouraging men with different viewpoints to compromise. Working from a plan proposed by Virginia's James Madison, the convention set the basic rules for American government as we know it today, skillfully balancing power between the government and the people; big states and small; the states and the nation; the president, the congress, and the courts.

Washington hoped that he could soon return to his retirement, but the delegates had other ideas, shaping the powerful new office of president of the United States with him in mind. As South Carolina delegate Pierce Butler admitted, "Many of the members cast their eyes towards General Washington as President; and shaped their ideas of the powers to be given to a president, by their opinions of his virtue."

Federalist Papers

Alexander Hamilton, working with James Madison and John Jay, wrote a series of newspaper columns called "The Federalist" that helped sway public opinion in favor of the Constitution.

After many compromises, the convention approved the Constitution on September 17. Washington almost didn't make it back to Mount Vernon. One of his carriage horses plunged through "an old, rotten, and long-disused bridge." Washington made it home safely, then awaited the outcome of another cliff-hanger—Would enough states vote to approve a new constitution that limited state power?

Except for a few letters to friends, Washington stayed out of the debate that raged through all 13 states, but many people came out in favor of the Constitution simply because they knew that the man they most trusted had been the first to sign it. Washington wasn't completely satisfied with some of the compromises that had gone into the Constitution, and he wasn't entirely thrilled with the likelihood that if it was approved he would be asked to be president. Still, when the necessary nine states had voted in favor, he wrote, "No one can rejoice more than I do at every step the people of this great country take to preserve the union, establish good order and government, and to render the nation happy at home and respectable abroad."

The Continental Congress, among its last acts before giving way to the new Senate and House of Representatives, chose New York as a new capital and scheduled elections. Presidential campaigns and political parties as we know them today did not yet exist. The states simply chose respected men for an Electoral College, which in turn voted on the best men for president and vice president. Washington never ran for president, but it was no surprise to anyone when he was again a unanimous choice. John Adams, who had led the movement for independence in Congress, was chosen as vice president.

When official word of the election reached Mount Vernon on April 14, 1789, Washington's bags had long since been packed. Humble as ever, he wrote Henry Knox, his old artillery commander, "My movements to the chair of Government will be accompanied with feelings not unlike those of a culprit who is going to the place of his execution."

The future president presides over the signing of the Constitution. Hamilton, Franklin, and Madison are seated front and center.

chapter 9

Mr. President

Washington kept diaries throughout his adult life. Mostly they are filled with plain facts—where he went, what he spent, who he met—but few if any thoughts or feelings. Not so upon departing to begin his term as president: "About ten o'clock I bade adieu to Mount Vernon, to private life, and to domestic felicity, and with a mind oppressed with more anxious and painful sensations than I have words to express, set out for New York…with the best dispositions to render service to my country in obedience to its call, but with less hope of answering its expectations." Martha, who had accompanied him to so many army camps,

Washington is rowed across the Hudson River to New York City by a crew of 13 oarsmen representing the original 13 states.

felt too depressed and over-whelmed to go with him.

At every stage of his eight-day journey Washington was greeted

PRECEDENT

An example that others may choose to follow in the future.

with crowds and pomp and pageantry, yet he remained uneasy when he reached Manhattan: "The display of boats which attended and joined us on this occasion, some with vocal and some with instrumental music on board; the decorations of the ships, the roar of cannon and the loud acclamations of the people, which rent [tore] the skies as I passed along the wharves, filled my mind with sensations as painful…as they are pleasing."

Everything the first president did would set a precedent, but first, what should people call him? Vice President Adams argued for "His Most Benign Highness," and a Senate committee called for "His Highness the President of the United States and Protector of the Rights of the Same." Washington would have none of that. He would be addressed simply as "Mr. President," and many continued to refer to him as "the General."

The president was inaugurated—officially sworn in—before the House and Senate on April 30, 1789. Back at Mount Vernon he had prepared a detailed 73-page speech, but he

"I bade adieu to Mount Vernon, to private life, and to domestic felicity."

—George Washington

Inauguration Ceremony

The Constitution says little about inaugurations other than making presidents take a 35-word oath to defend the Constitution. Washington added the words, "So help me God," and so far every president has followed his example. Washington also set the precedent of making a speech—an inaugural address—and holding celebrations, and the speeches and celebrations have been getting bigger ever since.

replaced this with a short address that said little about his plans. Pennsylvania senator William Maclay wrote, "This great man was agitated and embarrassed more than ever he was by the leveled cannon or pointed musket." Without mentioning God by name, the president appealed to "the great author of every public and private good," noting that "No people can be bound to acknowledge and adore the invisible hand which conducts the affairs of men more than the people of the United States."

As their terms began, President Washington turned to Vice President Adams for advice, but old personality clashes going back to the Revolution soon reopened. With no one interested in his strongly held opinions, Adams would tell his wife, Abigail, "My country has in its wisdom contrived for me the most insignificant office that ever the invention of man contrived or his imagination conceived."

Washington had no intention of running the country all by himself. Once Congress voted on a plan to organize the

CABINET

The heads or "secretaries" of important government departments serving together as advisers to a president or other leader.

government, Washington appointed his cabinet. Henry Knox was secretary of war. Alexander Hamilton, who had been one of Washington's top aides during the Revolution and was a founder of the Bank of New York, was secretary of the treasury. Washington offered the State Department, which oversaw foreign relations, to John Jay, but agreed to Jay's request to be named chief justice of the Supreme Court, instead. The president then named his fellow Virginian Thomas Jefferson, author of the Declaration of Independence, as secretary of state. Jefferson, who had been serving as minister to France, did not arrive in New York until the following year.

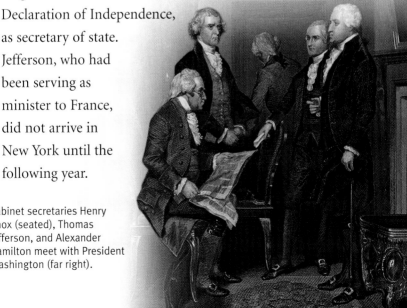

Cabinet secretaries Henry Knox (seated), Thomas Jefferson, and Alexander Hamilton meet with President Washington (far right).

A month into Washington's term, Martha arrived with Nelly and Wash. They, too, were given rousing welcomes all along the road to New York. "Dear Little Washington," Martha wrote of her grandson, "seemed to be lost in a maze at the great parade that was made for us all the way we came."

Washington was far too busy to let visitors drop in all the time at the rented Executive Mansion, so he set up a regular schedule of Thursday afternoon dinners for invited government officials. State dinners could be a trial. Senator Maclay recorded of one gathering, "It was the most solemn dinner ever I sat at. Not a health drank; scarce a word said until the cloth was taken away."

Any properly dressed gentleman could stop by for the presidential "levee" from three to four on Tuesdays. The first first lady hosted public receptions every Friday

As first lady, Martha Washington hosted formal receptions on Fridays at the Executive Mansion.

evening. Although their husbands did not get along very well, Abigail Adams quickly took to Martha, writing that "Mrs. Washington is one of those unassuming characters which create love and esteem." The president was usually stiff and ill-at-ease with the gentlemen at his Tuesday afternoon levees, but he lightened up and enjoyed himself with the ladies at Martha's receptions.

The Washingtons brought favorite slaves from Mount Vernon to attend them in New York, and then in Philadelphia when the

Martha Washington was 58 when she became America's first first lady.

capital moved there in 1790. Martha's maid Ona Judge was a darling of Philadelphia society and was often seen at the theater. Hercules, the Washingtons' cook, was so valued that he was allowed to sell off Executive Mansion leftovers to buy himself fine clothing. It was about as good a life as a slave could have, and the first family prided themselves on being benevolent masters, but the slaves still wished to be free.

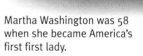

"Mrs. Washington is one of those unassuming characters which create love and esteem."

—Abigail Adams

Hercules ran away and was never heard from again. Ona escaped to Portsmouth, New Hampshire, after learning that Martha was planning to give her as a wedding present to a granddaughter. Martha, who seems to have shared none of Washington's misgivings about slavery, pressured him to recover Ona, and he made some halfhearted attempts to bring her back before giving up rather than risk a scandal.

Washington's first year in office went more smoothly than he had dared hope, although in June he needed painful surgery to remove a tumor, and in September he learned that his 81-year-old mother had died of cancer. The new government was up and running, however, and, apart from Adams, he felt very comfortable with his distinguished team of advisers.

Triumphal arches sprang up in Boston and other cities to celebrate the arrival of President Washington.

While Congress took a long recess in the fall of 1789, Washington took a monthlong tour of the New England states of Connecticut, Massachusetts, and

FEDERAL

Federal refers to the central, national government as compared with state or local government.

New Hampshire. (Vermont and Maine weren't states yet, and the president bypassed Rhode Island, which did not approve the Constitution until 1790.) He was greeted with feasts and parades in almost every town he visited, and this time he let himself enjoy the star treatment—it was a sign that the people thought he was doing a good job.

By the time Jefferson arrived at the State Department in March 1790, Treasury Secretary Hamilton had a plan for giving the new nation a firm financial foundation and paying off government debts from the Revolution. Hamilton proposed that the federal government, now that it could collect taxes, should assume responsibility for any war debts that the states still hadn't paid. States like Massachusetts that still had heavy debts were enthusiastic, but Virginia, which had already paid off most of its own, felt cheated. James Madison, now a powerful Virginia congressman, blocked Hamilton's plan.

Jefferson, too, had doubts about Hamilton's program, but he worked out a compromise with Madison that got it passed in Congress. Virginia's representatives went along with the northern delegations who already supported the

treasury secretary, and in return the northerners agreed to move the national capital south, first to Philadelphia for 10 years, and then to a new city to be built on the Potomac.

Washington personally selected the site for the new Federal City, later named Washington, D.C., a few miles up the Potomac from Mount Vernon.

Washington, who quietly supported both the Hamilton plan and building a new capital close to Mount Vernon, was very pleased. He made his last farewells to New York, returned home to Virginia for a short vacation, and arrived in Philadelphia in December 1790.

In 1791, Washington toured the Carolinas and Georgia, "To see with my own eyes the situation of the country and to learn on the spot the condition and disposition of our citizens." The president was appalled at the quality of the roads on his 1,887-mile journey, but he was pleased to see that "Tranquility reigns among the people, with that disposition towards the general government which is likely to preserve it."

That tranquility didn't last. Hamilton proposed creating a large national bank, part public and part private, that could lend money for important projects. Congress approved the proposal and Washington signed it, but Jefferson and Madison felt that it was a giveaway to rich northern moneymen. Washington valued the ideas of both Jefferson and Hamilton, but the increasingly personal disagreements between them divided the government into two rival factions.

Republicans and Democrats

The Republicans of Jefferson's time evolved into the Democratic Party of today. The modern Republican Party, founded in 1854, is unrelated to Jefferson's Republicans or Hamilton's Federalists.

The First Bank of the United States opened in 1797 and still stands as part of Philadelphia's Independence National Historic Park.

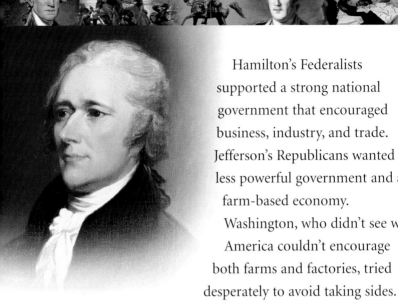

Hamilton's Federalists supported a strong national government that encouraged business, industry, and trade. Jefferson's Republicans wanted a less powerful government and a farm-based economy.

Washington, who didn't see why America couldn't encourage both farms and factories, tried desperately to avoid taking sides.

Alexander Hamilton was raised in poverty on the Caribbean island of St. Croix before becoming one of the most influential men in America.

Hamilton and Jefferson were also oceans apart on foreign policy. Hamilton's Federalists wanted closer ties and more trade with Britain. Jefferson thought that any friends of England were "monarchists" secretly plotting to install an American monarchy. His Republicans favored France, especially now that a revolution, with Lafayette among its leaders, had removed King Louis XVI from power.

Old friends became bitter enemies as Republicans and Federalists hurled insults and accusations at each other. Hamilton and Madison had worked closely together to get the Constitution written and approved, but now Hamilton complained that "Mr. Madison cooperating with Mr. Jefferson is at the head of a faction decidedly hostile to me and… dangerous to the union, peace, and happiness of the country."

The French Revolution

France had helped the United States to win liberty, and soon the French people demanded liberty for themselves. Louis XVI grudgingly agreed to share power, like the kings and queens of England, but he broke a series of promises. On July 14, 1789, angry citizens seized the Bastille, a towering prison in the heart of Paris, and within two years King Louis was a prisoner himself.

Jefferson told Washington he wanted to leave the cabinet, but that "I will not suffer my retirement to be clouded by the slanders of a man [Hamilton] whose history, from the moment at which history can stoop to notice him, is a tissue of machinations against the liberty of the country which has…heaped its honors on his head."

While Republicans and Federalists attacked each other in the newspapers, Washington told his cabinet that he was retiring, this time for good, at the end of his four-year term. He asked Madison to help him write a farewell address, but Madison refused.

Jefferson and Hamilton had finally found something they both agreed on: Only Washington could hold the country together. He would have to agree to stay on for another four years.

Thomas Jefferson, a wealthy Virginia aristocrat who became popular as a champion of the common man, would later be elected as the third president.

chapter **10**

Second Term

Washington tried to make peace between his feuding cabinet secretaries, telling Jefferson, "I have a great— a sincere esteem and regard for you both, and ardently wish that some line could be marked out by which both of you could walk." Still not committing himself to a second term, he pleaded with Hamilton and Jefferson to stay on and work for whomever the next president might be. Both insisted that they wanted out, but that they might grit their teeth and stay on if Washington did. On February 13, 1793, the Electoral College unanimously sentenced Washington to another four years of exile from Mount Vernon.

Washington was 62 at his second inauguration. His gloomy speech was a whopping two paragraphs long—the shortest inaugural address in history.

Washington hadn't looked forward to his first term

France's king Louis XVI prepares to meet the guillotine.

GUILLOTINE

A machine used in France during and after the revolution to chop off people's heads with a heavy falling blade.

either, but he'd still managed to take satisfaction in getting the new government off to a smooth start. The second term, however, was even worse than he'd feared, as an increasingly frail Washington faced one crisis after another.

The French Revolution remained enormously popular with the American people, even as it took a violent turn in 1793. Louis XVI lost his head to the guillotine, and thousands of executions followed. A horrified Hamilton was convinced that Jefferson wanted a similar Reign of Terror in America. Republican newspapers ridiculed anything "monarchist," including Washington's formal gatherings at the Executive Mansion, and some Republicans joked about guillotining Washington.

France and England were at war again. Washington wanted to stay out of it, but French ambassador Edmond Charles Genêt, encouraged by Jefferson's followers, went to work trying to draw the United States in. "Citizen" Genêt traveled from town to town,

French ambassador "Citizen" Genêt stirred up trouble as he tried to enlist America in a new war against Britain.

PRIVATEER

A pirate or pirate ship legally authorized by one country to attack the ships of an enemy country.

rousing crowds against Washington and his Neutrality Proclamation, in which the president had declared that America would not take sides between England and France.

Worse, Genêt commissioned American ships as privateers, giving them licenses to attack and seize English merchant ships. Washington had no desire to tangle with the powerful British navy, which was likely to combat the privateers by cracking down on all American shipping. Even Jefferson agreed that Genêt had gone too far. Before the cabinet could decide just how strongly they should protest to Genêt's government, France sent a less troublesome ambassador.

That summer in Philadelphia, something deadly was in the air. Washington noted in August 1793, "We are all well at present, but the city is very sickly and numbers dying

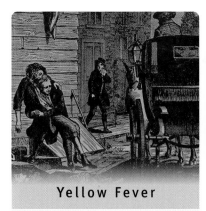

Yellow Fever

Yellow fever gives its victims' skin a yellowish tint while wracking them with high fevers and intense bloody vomiting. Caused by a virus and spread by mosquitoes, the disease probably stowed away to Philadelphia aboard ships from the Caribbean.

daily." Nobody understood what caused the mysterious yellow fever, but one in ten residents of America's largest city died that summer. The population shrunk from 40,000 to 20,000, as almost anyone who could afford to fled the epidemic.

Washington was torn. As a soldier, he had never hesitated to ride where bullets were flying, but he didn't want to endanger his family, and Martha and her grandchildren refused to leave without him. Hamilton was stricken with

AT a MEETING of the Corporation of the city of Burlington, August 30th, 1793, the following recommendations to the citizens was unanimously agreed to.

WHEREAS there is great reason for caution against the malignant Fever or contagious disorder, which prevails in Philadelphia, and it is our duty to use every probable means to prevent the same in the city of Burlington; the Corporation of Burlington after collecting every advice which could be obtained,

RECOMMEND to the Citizens of Burlington,

1. That all unnecessary intercourse be avoided with Philadelphia, that no dry goods, woollen cloths, woollens, cottons or linens, or any packages where straw, hay or shaving, are used, be imported within twenty days.

2. That the masters of the boats which ply to and from Burlington to Philadelphia, be very careful that they do not receive on board their vessels, or bring to this city within twenty days, any person or persons but those who appear in good health.

3. That no animal or vegetable substances be thrown or permitted to lay in the streets or alleys, but that all offals, water-melon rinds and substances that putrefy be thrown into the delaware or buried.

4. That no water be permitted to stagnate about the pumps, in the streets or near any houses ; but that the wharves, streets, alleys and gutters, ditches, house, and barnyards, be kept as clean as possible.

5. The Physicians in Burlington are requested to make report to the Mayor or Recorder as soon as possible, after they shall have been called to and visited any person or persons, who shall have the said malignant Fever.

Signed by order of the Corporation,

BOWES REED, Mayor.

The following means to prevent the contagion is recommended by the College of Physicians in Philadelphia.

" To avoid all fatigue of body and mind."

" To avoid standing or sitting in the sun, also in a current of air, or in the evening air."

" To accommodate the dress to the weather, and to exceed rather in warm than in cool cloathing."

" To avoid intemperance, but to use fermented liquors, such as wine, beer and cyder with moderation."

" The burning of gunpowder, the use of vinegar and camphor upon handkerchiefs or in smelling bottles, particularly by persons whose duty calls them to visit or attend the sick."

Published by order of the Corporation,

ABRAHAM GARDINER, Clerk.

Doctors did their best to fight yellow fever, but, not knowing its true cause, they couldn't stop it from spreading.

the fever and narrowly cheated death. It was hard to get much done when almost everyone who remained behind was either sick or scared to go outdoors.

Washington knew his presence calmed the people who stayed to brave the epidemic, but he reluctantly left in September on a previously scheduled vacation to Mount Vernon. It wasn't much of a holiday. There was no telling when it would be safe to return to Philadelphia, and a lot of government business followed Washington home. The most

A mob attacks a tax collector with tar and feathers during the Whiskey Rebellion.

satisfying part of his break was a visit to the site of the new capital city that had already been named for him. There was a ceremony as Washington laid the cornerstone of the Capitol building.

The plague of yellow fever vanished when fall weather turned cold. A hundred years would pass before doctors understood that the disease was spread by mosquitoes. Against the advice of his friends, Washington returned to Philadelphia.

Hamilton, after his slow recovery from the fever, decided he wasn't ready to leave Washington's cabinet just yet, but Jefferson resigned at the end of the year. It was bad news for the president. Jefferson and Hamilton hated each other, but

DEMOCRATIC

Responsible to the entire population, not just one class or group.

Washington had been able to strike a balance and find what was best in their conflicting ideas. Now that balance was gone, and Hamilton dominated the cabinet.

Once Jefferson was out of the government, he attacked Hamilton more freely than ever. Jefferson's allies formed groups called the Democratic Societies to campaign against what they saw as an increasingly aristocratic federal government and its taxes.

Hamilton's plan for paying national debts had included a tax on whiskey. It was accepted by the same New Englanders who had been up in arms over King George's tax on tea. But on the western frontier, where just about every farmer traded in homemade whiskey, people didn't take kindly to the taxman. Armed bands attacked government agents near Pittsburgh and, stirred up by the Democratic Societies, talked of raising their own army to march on Philadelphia or even start a new country.

President Washington, in general's uniform once more, reviews the army raised to put down the Whiskey Rebellion.

The growing Whiskey Rebellion had the frontier in turmoil.

Washington sent a warning to the rebels, then called up an army of almost 13,000 militiamen. He had no problem finding enough volunteers—even the Democratic Society of Pennsylvania demanded that the rebels obey the law. Washington and Hamilton got back in uniform to lead the army, but the rebels dispersed without a fight. Washington pardoned their leaders and sent the militiamen home despite Hamilton's urging to keep them together as a permanent national army.

Trouble with France had eased up with Genêt's dismissal, but trouble with England got worse. The British decreed that, as long as they were at war with France, any American ships caught trading with France could be captured and their crews forced to join the Royal Navy. Washington sent Chief Justice Jay to London to negotiate a peaceful solution.

Jay was gone for almost a year, and Washington was disappointed with the treaty he finally

John Jay served as one of America's top diplomats and as the first chief justice of the Supreme Court.

sent home. The Jay Treaty avoided war with England only by restricting American trade and conceding that England had the right to seize ships carrying French goods.

Angry Republican mobs hanged and burned images of John Jay to protest a treaty that they felt unfairly favored England over France.

The once decisive Washington couldn't make up his mind whether to sign the deeply flawed treaty, or risk war by rejecting it. Hamilton and Knox had both left the cabinet, and the president didn't have any confidence in their replacements. Edmund Randolph, who as attorney general had been Washington's chief legal adviser, and who had replaced Jefferson as secretary of state, told him to keep the treaty secret as long as possible.

In the end, Washington sent the treaty on to the Senate without recommending it one way or the other, then signed it after the senators approved it. There were massive protests once details of the Jay Treaty were finally published, and Washington's popularity was about as low as it had gotten during the worst days of the revolution. Encouraged by Jefferson, Republican newspapers wrote that Washington's presidency "has been a series of errors or of crimes."

Edmund Randolph served in Washington's cabinet, first as attorney general, and then as secretary of state.

Washington, who had always looked for and relied on good advisers, was starved for them now. Madison had become a fierce Republican follower of Jefferson. The only one the president still trusted was Randolph, and that changed when rival cabinet secretaries produced evidence suggesting that Randolph had been bribed by French agents. Randolph, who was almost certainly innocent, resigned angrily when Washington confronted him about the accusation.

Serving with Washington had becoming so unappealing that five different men turned down offers of Randolph's post as secretary of state. The president finally got his cabinet filled, but there wasn't a single man in it that he felt he could rely on.

Washington was showing signs of age. He often found that he had no memory of discussions his aides insisted he had taken part in. "I got such a wrench in my back" riding his horse near the Potomac, he wrote, that it took months before he could get back in the saddle without pain, yet when he rode in his carriage instead of walking or going on horseback, Republicans took it as one more sign that he was out of touch with the people and mocked "apish mimicry of kingship."

Many Federalists asked Washington to consider a third term. He flat out refused, and he also refused to take sides in the election of 1796. The Federalists backed Adams in the Electoral College, and he narrowly beat out Jefferson, who, under the terms of the Constitution, became vice president. Adams told his wife, Abigail, how even at the new president's inauguration, all eyes were on the departing Washington. "He seemed to enjoy a triumph over me. Methought I heard him say, 'Ay! I am fairly out and you fairly in! See which of us will be happiest!'…In the chamber of the House of Representatives was…I believe scarcely a dry eye but Washington's."

By voluntarily retiring, Washington performed one last great service to his country: He set the precedent that America's presidents do not serve for life.

Washington grew weary of the endless stream of artists who came to paint his portrait, though he dutifully sat for all of them. Perhaps Washington's least favorite painter was Gilbert Stuart, whose unflattering portrait is the basis for the image on the dollar bill.

chapter 11

Retirement

When the Washingtons returned to Mount Vernon in March 1797, the road home was lined with the same fanfare that had greeted them when Washington first took office. "The attentions we met with on our journey were very flattering," Washington wrote, "but I avoided in every instance where I…could…all parade or escorts."

The manor house and farms at Mount Vernon were in sad shape: "I have not one [building] or scarcely anything else about me that does not require considerable repairs."

He threw his energies into fixing the place up: "I am already surrounded by joiners, masons,

Washington shows plans for the new capital to Martha and her grandchildren, Wash and Nelly.

painters, etc....I have scarcely a room to put a friend into or to set in myself without the music of hammers or the odoriferous smell of paint."

Restoring Mount Vernon was expensive, and, as usual, Washington was short on cash and had to borrow. Though his frontier properties had skyrocketed in value, selling those faraway holdings took time. He did own assets that he could have easily sold for thousands of dollars, but he had long since resolved never to sell this "certain species of property which I possess very repugnantly to my own feelings"—his slaves.

Washington grew up taking slavery for granted, but his feelings had greatly evolved, in contrast with such fellow Virginians as Jefferson and Madison—and Martha, who couldn't understand why Ona Judge would be so ungrateful as to run away. Washington mostly kept his growing disgust with slavery to himself, and he held onto his slaves up to the very end. Part of his reluctance was patriotic—during the Revolution and the Constitutional Convention, divisions over slavery had threatened the union, as they someday would during the Civil War.

Part was personal—about half of the 316 slaves Washington held or rented at his death belonged to Martha or to her grandchildren as part of the Custis family estate. These "dower" slaves were not legally Washington's to free, yet many Custis slaves had intermarried with his own. Washington also felt that it would be irresponsible to free his

> *"I am not insensible to my declination in other respects."*
>
> —George Washington

slaves without helping them to find a way to support themselves. He didn't have the cash to make his slaves paid workers, and though he tried to convince English farmers to rent the Mount Vernon farms and hire his blacks as farmhands, there were no takers.

While Washington wrestled with private dilemmas, public life wouldn't leave him in peace. The Jay Treaty had mended relations with Britain only to damage them with France. Britain stopped its harassment of U.S. shipping, but now French privateers attacked so many American ships that captains refused to sail and many businesses went broke. When France threatened all-out war in 1798, many Federalists wanted Alexander Hamilton to lead a 10,000-man army. Instead President Adams, who didn't trust Hamilton, asked Washington to put on his uniform one more time.

The old general agreed to serve as commander in chief, but he was no longer up to the demands of the job. He chose Hamilton, Knox, and South Carolina's Charles Pinckney as his major generals, but he kept changing his mind about which one should be his second in command. At different times he nominated each of them for the position, and his memory had gotten so bad that he couldn't keep track of what he'd said to whom. President Adams was aghast when Washington finally settled on Hamilton.

Washington became obsessed with the design of his new uniform and was frustrated when his tailor, unable to find all the gold thread Washington wanted, sent the uniform to Europe to be completed. It wasn't ready in time for Nelly Custis's wedding on Washington's sixty-seventh birthday, February 22, 1799, or for July Fourth celebrations that summer. France backed away from its threats before the new army that had caused so much stress was even called up, and Washington never wore the uniform.

Washington was repeatedly asked to come out of retirement once again to seek the presidency in the 1800 election, but he responded, "Although I have abundant cause to be thankful for the good health with which I am blessed, yet I am not insensible to my declination in other respects. It would be criminal therefore in me, although it should be the wish of my Countrymen, and I could be elected, to accept an Office under this conviction, which another would discharge with more ability."

Rembrandt Peale, whose father, Charles Wilson Peale, painted the earliest known portrait of Washington, was only 17 when he painted the aging leader himself.

12

Last Battle

December 12, 1799. George Washington is making his daily inspection of his Mount Vernon farms when a winter storm blows in. It's not nearly as bad as the one he braved crossing the Delaware in 1776, but Washington is a lot older. Ignoring the weather, he rides for about five hours through snow and hail and rain.

Next day, Washington has a sore throat. His secretary, Tobias Lear, suggests some medicine, but the old general says, "You know I never take anything for a cold. Let it go as it came." His voice is hoarse, but he stays cheerful, except when James

Those present at Washington's deathbed all agreed that he remained calm and brave to the very end.

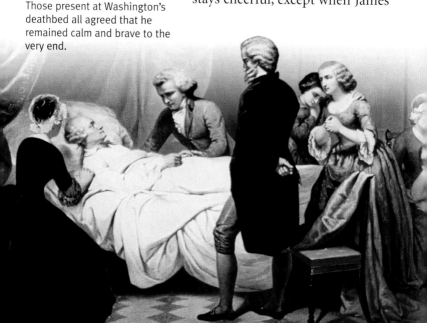

Madison comes up in a discussion of Virginia politics.

In the middle of the night, Washington wakes Martha. He can hardly speak or breath, but he insists she stay with him rather than risk catching cold herself fetching a servant. In the morning, Washington insists on the standard medical treatment of having some of his blood drained even before his old friend, Dr. James Craik, can arrive. Martha fears that too much blood is being taken, but Washington gasps, "More, more."

One of Washington's doctors is said to have cut the pendulum on this bedroom clock, stopping it forever at the time of the great man's death.

Washington finds it harder and harder to breathe. Three doctors try their best remedies, from "blister of cantharides" (a medicine made from dried beetles) to gargling vinegar to still more bleeding, but nothing helps. The patient remains calm, giving final instructions to his wife and secretary. "Do you understand me?" he rasps, and when Lear tells him yes, the old general breathes his last words: "'Tis well."

About 10:20 the night of December 14, Washington calmly feels his own pulse; then his hand falls to his side. "Is he gone?" asks Martha, and Lear silently holds up his own hand "as a signal that he was no more."

chapter 13

The Man and the Monument

In keeping with his will, Washington was interred in the old family tomb at Mount Vernon. Although he had asked to be entombed "in a private manner, without parade or funeral oration," hundreds of mourners showed up to a service led by four ministers, while a ship on the Potomac fired off artillery salutes. As word of Washington's death slowly spread from town to town, the nation went into mourning. First Lady Abigail Adams wrote to her sister that "No man ever lived more deservedly beloved and respected." Shops and theaters were closed. Thousands turned out for memorial gatherings throughout

Washington rises from his tomb through a shaft of heavenly light in this best-selling print by John James Barralet.

In 1831, the remains of George and Martha Washington were moved to a new tomb at Mount Vernon.

the nation. So many people dressed in black that many shops were sold out of black clothing for the next six months.

Paintings from 1800 showed angels lifting a blissful Washington up to heaven. Mason L. Weems, writing the first popular biography of Washington that year, wrote, "Swift on angel's wings, the brightening saint ascended." It was Parson Weems who invented the cherry tree story and other legends that came to be better known than the real George Washington.

Washington was no saint. He was more honest than the average leader, but it was far from true that he couldn't tell a lie; without his great skill at deceiving the British, the American Revolution might have failed. Washington was no military genius, and he lost many more battles than he won, but it is the rare general indeed who could have kept the ragged Continental army together year after year to outlast the most powerful army in the world.

George Washington Parke Custis, Martha's last surviving grandchild, wrote a popular memoir about his stepgrandfather.

Washington made his fair share of blunders, yet he learned from them and kept on trying to do better. His letters could be downright whiny about the problems he faced, yet he never gave up. He was far from selfless, yet he resisted all temptation to become a king or a dictator. He was hard to get close to, yet he was a good listener, and he kept people working together who had little in common other than their respect for his leadership.

We can wish that Washington had shown more leadership on the issue of slavery, but we can also respect the way his views changed over time. Jefferson and Madison often expressed regret about slavery, but of all the Virginia founding fathers, only Washington freed his slaves. Washington's will, signed six months before his death, gave his valet William Lee "immediate freedom" and a generous yearly pension "for his faithful services during the Revolutionary War." The rest of his slaves were to be freed following Martha's death. For any

Eleanor "Nelly" Parke Custis married George Washington's nephew Lawrence Lewis and bore eight children.

"who from old age or bodily infirmities" or too young "that will be unable to support themselves, it is my will and desire that [they] shall be comfortably clothed and fed by my heirs while they live." Washington was ahead of his time in insisting that the freed blacks "be taught to read and write," a practice that Virginia soon outlawed.

Parson Weems' Fable

Artist Grant Wood pokes fun at stories about Washington in this 1939 painting. Biographer Mason Weems reveals Gus Washington confronting his son about the fallen cherry tree. Little George, hatchet in hand, has the face of the old man on the dollar bill.

Martha didn't wait for her own death to carry out her husband's wishes. Fearing that George's slaves might want to harm her in order to liberate themselves more quickly, she freed all 123 on January 1, 1801. Her own slaves were divided among her grandchildren after her death on May 22, 1802, and only a few Custis family slaves saw freedom before the bloody Civil War of the 1860s. Leading the Confederate forces dedicated to preserve the South's slaveholding way of life was General Robert E. Lee, who in 1831 had married Martha's great-granddaughter Mary Custis.

The Civil War probably wouldn't have come as a terrible shock to Washington. An English traveler reported that in

Washington first appeared on the dollar bill in 1869 and on the quarter in 1932.

1798 Washington had told him that he could "clearly foresee that nothing but the rooting out of slavery can perpetuate the existence of our union." Both Northern and Southern armies left Mount Vernon in peace during the Civil War, but Thomas Jefferson reported that Washington had said that if the North and South should split up, "he had made up his mind to move and be of the northern." However much Washington loved Mount Vernon, the state of Virginia held less of a claim on him than the United States of America. He did as much as anyone to unite the states as a nation and establish a republic built to last through the centuries.

In the fall of 1800, the federal government left Philadelphia for the new capital that Washington had planned. John Adams moved into the mansion that would later be called the White House. He and Abigail only lived there a few months before Thomas Jefferson was voted in as the third president.

Congress had a magnificent tomb built right in the heart of the new Capitol building to house the earthly remains of the man Congressman Henry "Lighthorse Harry" Lee called "First in war, first in peace, and first in the hearts of his countrymen." Washington's family honored the first president's wishes and kept his bones at Mount Vernon, leaving the tomb at the Capitol empty to this day. But the capital that Washington gave his name to has grown even beyond his dreams, as has the nation he did so much for.

Our national capital, the 42nd state, and at least 21 American mountains, 31 counties, 277 communities, and thousands of streets, bridges, highways, schools, stores, and businesses are all monuments to the man known in his own lifetime as the father of his country. Though Washington died in the last days of the eighteenth century, the things that he did and the things he chose not to do still echo through our lives in the twenty-first.

The Washington Monument rises 555 feet to tower above the nation's capital. The monument was first proposed in Congress within days of Washington's death, but work wasn't begun until 1848 and wasn't completed until 1888.

Washington Slept Here

Apart from his voyage to Barbados in 1751, George Washington never left the United States that he did so much to help shape. Still, Washington got around far more than most other Americans. Between his military career, his surveying expeditions, and his presidential tours of the north and south, Washington visited all thirteen original states plus the future states of West Virginia, which he first surveyed in 1748; Ohio, where he visited a Mingo Indian village near present-day Steubenville in 1770; and Maine, where he went fishing off Kittery in 1789.

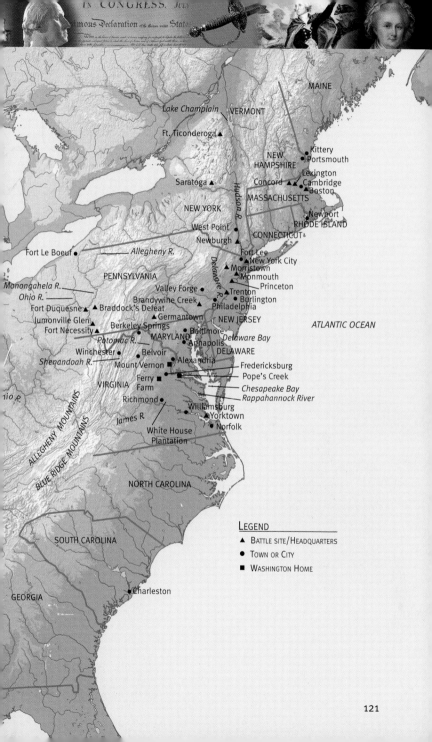

MAINE

Lake Champlain   VERMONT

Ft. Ticonderoga ▲

NEW HAMPSHIRE
Kittery
Portsmouth

Concord ▲ Lexington
Cambridge
Boston

Saratoga ▲

MASSACHUSETTS

NEW YORK

Hudson R.

West Point ▲
Newburgh ▲

Newport
RHODE ISLAND

CONNECTICUT

Fort Le Boeuf ●   *Allegheny R.*

Fort Lee ▲
New York City ●
Morristown ▲
Princeton ▲
Monmouth ▲

Delaware R.

PENNSYLVANIA

Monongahela R.
Ohio R.

Valley Forge ●
Trenton ▲
Burlington ●

Fort Duquesne ▲ ▲ Braddock's Defeat
Jumonville Glen ▲
Fort Necessity ▲

Brandywine Creek ▲
Philadelphia ●

▲ Germantown
Berkeley Springs ●

NEW JERSEY

ATLANTIC OCEAN

Potomac R.
MARYLAND
Baltimore ●

Delaware Bay

Winchester ●
Belvoir ●

Annapolis ●
DELAWARE

Shenandoah R.

Mount Vernon ■
Alexandria ■

Fredericksburg
Pope's Creek

ilo R.

VIRGINIA

Ferry
Farm ■

Chesapeake Bay
Rappahannock River

ALLEGHENY MOUNTAINS

Richmond ●

Williamsburg
Yorktown ▲
Norfolk ●

James R.

BLUE RIDGE MOUNTAINS

White House
Plantation

NORTH CAROLINA

LEGEND

▲ BATTLE SITE/HEADQUARTERS
● TOWN OR CITY
■ WASHINGTON HOME

SOUTH CAROLINA

GEORGIA   Charleston ●

Events in the Life of George Washington

January 6, 1759
George marries Martha Dandridge Custis and settles at Mount Vernon with Martha and her two children.

February 22, 1732
George Washington is born in Westmoreland County, Virginia.

May–July 1754
Washington's ambush of French Ensign Jumonville and defeat at Fort Necessity are the first skirmishes in the French and Indian War.

July 4, 1776
The Declaration of Independence is signed.

April 19, 1775
Fighting at Lexington and Concord, Massachusetts, begins the American Revolution.

September 1751– July 26, 1752
Washington accompanies brother Lawrence to Barbados and survives smallpox, but Lawrence dies of tuberculosis at Mount Vernon.

July 3, 1775
Washington takes command of the Continental army at Cambridge, Massachusetts.

March–April 1748
Washington joins George William Fairfax on a surveying expedition in the Shenandoah Valley.

December 16, 1773
Boston Tea Party

December 1777–June 1778
Washington and his army
winter at Valley Forge.

August–December 1776
Washington's army is
driven out of New York
and New Jersey.

April 30, 1789
Washington is inaugurated
as the first president.

**September–
October 1794**
The Whiskey
Rebellion

September, 1783
Treaty of Paris

December 25–26, 1776
Washington leads troops
across the Delaware River to
defeat the Hessians at Trenton.

November 25, 1783
The British leave
New York.

September 17, 1787
Washington is first to
sign the Constitution.

October 19, 1781
Cornwallis's army
surrenders at Yorktown.

December 14, 1799
George Washington
dies at Mount
Vernon.

Bibliography

The American Revolution: Writings from the War of Independence. Selected by John H. Rhodehamel. New York: Library of America, 2001.

Commager, Henry Steele, and Richard B. Morris. *The Spirit of 'Seventy-Six: The Story of the American Revolution as Told by Participants.* Bicentennial Edition. New York: Harper, 1975.

Dann, John C., ed. *The Revolution Remembered : Eyewitness Accounts of the War for Independence.* Chicago: University of Chicago Press, 1980.

Davis, Kenneth C. *Don't Know Much About History.* New York: Avon, 1995.

Fields, Joseph E., ed. *Worthy Partner: The Papers of Martha Washington.* Westport, CT: Greenwood, 1994.

Fischer, David Hackett. *Washington's Crossing.* New York: Oxford, 2004

Flexner, James Thomas. *George Washington: The Forge of Experience (1732-1775).* Boston: Little, Brown, 1965. [GW: 1]

—. *George Washington in the American Revolution (1775-1783).* Boston: Little, Brown, 1968. [GW: 2]

—. *George Washington and the New Nation (1783-1793).* Boston: Little, Brown, 1970. [GW: 3]

—. *George Washington: Anguish and Farewell (1793-1799).* Boston: Little, Brown, 1972. [GW: 4]

—. *Washington: The Indispensable Man.* Boston: Little, Brown, 1974.

Lewis, Thomas A. Lewis. *For King and Country: The Maturing of George Washington, 1748-1760.* New York: HarperCollins, 1993.

Maclay, William. *Journal Of William Maclay, United States Senator From Pennsylvania 1789-1791.* Edited By Edgar S. Maclay. New York: Appleton, 1890. [Online at www.constitution.org/ac/maclay/journal.htm]

McDougall, Walter A. *Freedom Just Around the Corner.* New York: HarperCollins, 2004.

Niemcewicz, Julian Ursyn. *Under Their Vine and Fig Tree: Travels through America in 1797-1799, 1805.* Translated and edited by Metchie J. E. Budka. Elizabeth, NJ: Grassman, 1965.

Rosenfeld, Richard. *American Aurora.* New York: St. Martin's, 1997.

Schwartz, Barry. *George Washington: The Making of an American Symbol.* New York: Free Press, 1987.

Washington, George. *A Biography in His Own Words.* Edited by Ralph K. Andrist. New York: Newsweek, 1972.

—. *Writings.* Selected by John H. Rhodehamel. New York: Library of America, 1997. [LOA]

Wheeler, Richard. *Voices of 1776.* New York: Crowell, 1972.

Wiencek, Henry. *An Imperfect God: George Washington, His Slaves, and the Creation of America.* New York: Farrar, Strauss & Giroux, 2003.

Works Cited

Note: Spelling and punctuation have been modernized for easier reading.

12-13: "Rules of Civility" LOA, 3-10.

17: "Troublesome passion…" Letter to "Robin," circa 1749-1750, LOA, 16.

17: "Lays bleeding every hour…" Washington quoted in Flexner, GW:1, 43.

17-18: "So many important events…" Letter of 5/16/1798, LOA, 1003.

24: "I heard bullets whistle…" Letter of 5/31/1754, LOA, 48.

26: "The most infamous…" John Huske quoted in Flexner, GW: 1, 107.

28: "Seized with violent fevers…" Letter of 6/28/1755, LOA, 54.

30: "The supplicating tears…" Letter of 4/22/1756, LOA, 75.

34: "A Tunbridge tea set…" Washington quoted in Flexner, GW:1, 262.

34: "Generous and attentive." Washington quoted in Flexner, GW:1, 261.

34: "She rose from dinner…" Letter of 6/20/1773, LOA, 146.

34: "My anxiety to have him fit…" Letter of 5/30/1768, LOA, 127.

35: "I never did in my life…" Boucher quoted in Flexner, GW:1, 266.

37: "General Washington treats his slaves…" Niemcewicz, 100-101.

39: "To be made of the best seasoned wood…" Letter of 6/6/1768, LOA, 127.

41: "At a time when our lordly masters…" Letter of 4/5/1769, LOA, 130.

43: "The shot heard round the world." This famous phrase comes from Ralph Waldo Emerson's poem "Concord Hymn" (1837).

44: "I beg it may be remembered…" Address to Continental Congress, 6/16/1775, LOA, 167.

44: "You may believe me my dear Patsy…" Letter of 6/18/1775, LOA, 168. Martha burned her correspondence with Washington after his death, and this is one of only a handful of surviving letters to her.

46: Camp Chaos: Israel Trask quoted in Dann, *The Revolution Remembered*, 408-409.

47: "Their officers generally speaking…" Letter of 8/20/1775, LOA, 184.

49: "To put a speedy end …" George III speech of 10/26/1775, quoted in Commager, 254.

49: "A tyrant and his diabolical ministry." Letter of 2/10/1776, LOA, 214.

53: "I do declare…" Daniel McCurtin quoted in Flexner, GW:2, 95.

55: "Weak to the last degree." Lee quoted in Commager, 500.

55: "I think the game…" Letter of 12/10/1776, LOA, 260.

56: "Despair of surprising the town…" Letter of 12/27/1776, LOA, 262

57: "My brave fellows…" "Sergeant R." quoted in Commager, 519.

58: Chapter title from Thomas Paine's *The American Crisis*, quoted in *The American Revolution*, 238.

61: "He might have cut to pieces..." John Adams quoted from *The Adams Papers*, II:264, in Rosenfeld, 335.

62: "Poor food..." Albigence Waldo quoted in *The American Revolution*, 401.

65: "Swore...till the leaves shook on the trees." General Charles Scott quoted in Wheeler, 269.

69: "It would have been a less painful circumstance..." Letter of 4/30/1781, LOA, 420.

72: "During a tremendous cannonade..." John Suddarth quoted in Dann, 239.

73: "Marched out beating ..." Sarah Osborn quoted in Dann, 245

73: "The World Turned Upside Down." See "Comments on a March Allegedly Played by the British at Yorktown, 1781" by Arthur Schrader (www.colonial-music.org/Resource/Schrader.htm).

74: "For it will not be believed..." Letter of 2/6/1783, LOA, 484.

75: "A country that tramples..." John Armstrong quoted in *The American Revolution*, 775.

76: "Open the floodgates of civil discord..." Speech of 3/15/1783, LOA, 500.

76: "Made a short pause..." Samuel Shaw quoted in *The American Revolution*, 788.

77: "To pass the remainder of my life..." Circular letter of 6/8/1783, LOA, 516.

78: "My Dear Marquis..." Letter of 2/1/1784, LOA, 553.

79: "May be compared to a well-resorted tavern..." Letter of 2/15/1787, LOA, 638.

82: "Something must be done..." Letter of 5/18/1786, LOA, 600.

82: "Having happily assisted..." Letter of 8/15/1786, LOA, 607.

83: "Many of the members..." Pierce Butler quoted in Flexner, GW: 3, 134.

84: "An old, rotten..." Diary entry of 9/19/1787, found at lcweb2.loc.gov/ammem/gwhtml/gwhome.html.

84: "No one can rejoice more than I..." Letter of 6/29/1788, LOA, 688.

85: "My movements to the chair..." Letter of 4/1/1789, LOA, 726.

86: "About ten o'clock I bade adieu..." Diary entry of 4/16/1789, LOA, 730.

87: "The display of boats..." Diary entry of 4/23/1789, LOA, 730.

88: "This great man..." Diary entry of 4/30/1789, Maclay, 9.

88: "The great author..." First Inaugural Address, 4/30/1789, LOA, 731.

88: "My country has in its wisdom..." John Adams, letter of 12/19/1793.

90: "Dear Little Washington..." Letter of 6/8/1789, Fields, 215.

90: "It was the most solemn dinner..." Diary entry of 8/27/1789, Maclay, 138.

91: "Mrs. Washington is..." Abigail Adams, letter of 7/12/1789.

94: "To see with my own eyes..." Letter of 11/14/1791, LOA, 795.

94: "Tranquility reigns..." Letter of 7/20/1791, LOA, 777.

96: "Mr. Madison cooperating..." Alexander Hamilton, letter of 5/26/1792.

97: "I will not suffer..." Thomas Jefferson, letter of 9/9/1792.

98: "I have a great—a sincere esteem..." Letter of 10/18/1792, LOA, 826.

100: "We are all well at present..." Letter of 8/25/1793, quoted in Flexner, GW:4, 85.

105: "Has been a series of errors..." *Philadelphia Aurora*, 9/18/1795, quoted in Rosenfeld, 30.

106: "I got such a wrench in my back" Washington quoted in Flexner, GW: 4, 156.

107: "Apish mimicry of kingship." *Philadelphia Aurora*, 9/11/1795, quoted in Rosenfeld, 29.

107: "He seemed to enjoy..." John Adams, letter of 3/5/1797.

108: "The attentions we met..." Letter of 4/3/1797, LOA, 993.

108: "I have not one..." Letter of 4/3/1797, LOA, 993.

109: "Certain species of property..." Letter of 5/6/1794, LOA, 868.

111: "Although I have abundant cause..." Letter of 7/21/1799, LOA, 1044.

112-113: Quotes taken from "Tobias Lear's Journal Account of George Washington's Last Illness and Death," found at gwpapers.virginia.edu/exhibits/mourning/lear.html.

114: "In a private manner..." Last will and testament, 7/19/1799, LOA, 1035.

114: "No man ever lived..." Abigail Adams, letter of 12/22/1799.

115: "Swift on angel's wings..." Mason L. Weems, *The Life of George Washington*, found at xroads.virginia.edu/~CAP/gw/chap12.html

116-117: "For his faithful services..." and other quotes from Washington's will, LOA, 1023.

118: "Clearly foresee that nothing..." John Bernard quoted in Flexner, GW: 4, 485.

118: "He had made up his mind..." Thomas Jefferson quoted in Flexner, GW: 4, 482

119: "First in war..." Henry "Lighthorse Harry" Lee, speech to Congress, 12/26/1799.

For Further Study

Washington's lovingly maintained home and farms at Mount Vernon are open to the public every day. Fascinating photos, information, and up-to-the-minute research are available online at **www.mountvernon.org**.

The National Park Service (**www.nps.gov**) maintains many of the historic sites described in this book, including Washington's birthplace, Fort Necessity, Independence National Historic Park, Valley Forge, Yorktown Battlefield, and the Washington Monument.

The Library of Congress maintains an online collection of about 65,000 letters, diaries, notes, and other documents penned by Washington at **lcweb2.loc.gov/ammem/gwhtml/gwhome.html**.

Index

Acknowledgments

My deepest thanks to Mary V. Thompson, research specialist at the Mount Vernon Ladies' Association, for her thoughtful comments and advice; to endlessly patient Beth Hester and Beth Sutinis of DK; and especially to Laaren and the girls for putting up with all the late nights and schlepping along to all those historic sites. I can't tell a lie—you're the greatest.

Picture Credits

Northwind Picture Archives: pp.5,6-7,11t,14,15,17,22,27 28,29,33,46,47,50,51, 52b,56,57,62,66,67,86, 99,106,122tl, 122bl,123tl,123tr,124-125,126-127. Virginia Tourism: pp.11b,13. George Washington Masonic National Memorial: p.16. Corbis: pp.21,49,65,78,91,100,116t,116b Bettman; p.25 Ted Spiegel; p.19,31 Royalty Free; pp.34-35b Richard T.Nowitz; p.38 Stapleton Collection; pp.52t,122tr Joseph Sohm/ChromoSohm Inc.; pp.72,123bl PoodlesRock; pp.92,94,95, 97,100, 103,112 Corbis; pp.98 Leonard de Selva; p.107 Museum of the City of New York; p.115 Todd Gipstein; p.118 Joseph Sohm/Visions of America; p.119 Wolfgang Kaehler. National Park Service: pp.23 Fred Threlfall; p.24. Bridgeman Art Library: p.26 State Hist.Soc.of Wisconsin; pp.36,53,82,96 New York Historical Society; p.40 Scottish National Portrait Gallery;p.45 National Museum of American Art/ Smithsonian Institute; p.55 The Classical Gallery/Virginia; p.60 Massachusetts Historical Society; pp.61,88 Delaware Art Museum; p.63 Pennsylvania State Capitol; p.64 Bibliotheque Nationale Archives Charmet/Paris; p.70 Guildhall Art Gallery/London;p.90 Brooklyn Museum of Art; p.111 The Detroit Institute of Arts; p.117 Christie's Images/London. Washington & Lee University: pp.32,35tr. Ohio Historical Society: p.37. Library of Congress: pp.39,42,43,122br. Adams Historical Society: p.44. Colonial Williamsburg Foundation: p.54. Getty Images: pp.58,59,68 Hulton Archive. Art Resource: pp.69 Réunion des Musées Nationaux; pp.74,104 Smithsonian American Art Museum;p.77 Scala; pp.85,89,102 Art Resource; p.123br SEF. Granger Collection: pp.75,101,105,108. Mt.Vernon Ladies Association: pp.76,80,81,113. U.S. Mint: p.118(coin). Winterthur Museum:p.114. **Border photos**, from left to right Colonial Williamsburg Foundation; Mt. Vernon Ladies Association; Art Resource/ SEF; Mt. Vernon Ladies Association; Colonial Williamsburg Foundation; Mt.Vernon Ladies Association; Mt. Vernon Ladies Association; Art Resource/The Pierpont Morgan Library; Mt.Vernon Ladies Association; Mt. Vernon Ladies Association; Mt. Vernon Ladies Association. All other images copyright © DK Images.

About the Author

Lenny Hort has written such popular books as *The Seals on the Bus*, a School Library Journal Best Book of the Year, and *How Many Stars in the Sky?*, a PBS Reading Rainbow book. He lives with his wife, Laaren Brown, and their daughters, Sophie, Irene, and Phoebe, in Fort Lee, New Jersey, where Washington and his army narrowly escaped from the British. To research this book the Horts traveled to Mount Vernon, Morristown, Newburgh, Fredericksburg, and other Washington-related sites.

Other DK Biographies you may enjoy:

DK Biography: *Abraham Lincoln*
by Tanya Lee Stone
ISBN 0-7566-0341-2 paperback
ISBN 0-7566-0490-7 hardcover

DK Biography: *Helen Keller*
by Leslie Garrett
ISBN 0-7566-0339-0 paperback
ISBN 0-7566-0488-5 hardcover

DK Biography: *Anne Frank*
by Kem Knapp Sawyer
ISBN 0-7566-0341-2 paperback
ISBN 0-7566-0490-7 hardcover

DK Biography: *John F. Kennedy*
by Howard S. Kaplan
ISBN 0-7566-0340-4 paperback
ISBN 0-7566-0489-3 hardcover

DK Biography: *Martin Luther King, Jr.*
by Amy Pastan
ISBN 0-7566-0342-0 paperback
ISBN 0-7566-0491-5 hardcover

Look what the critics are saying about DK Biography!

"…highly readable, worthwhile overviews for young people…"—*Booklist*

"This new series from the inimitable DK Publishing brings together the usual brilliant photography with a historian's approach to biography subjects."
—*Ingram Library Services*